THE RAPTURE
PART II

**Fulfillment of: The Signs in The Sky,
The Festivals in Summer,
and The Parables of The End Times**

Rev. Jopie Rattu, Ph.D.
Sridadi Atiyanto, Ph.D.
Yunus Ciptawilangga, M.B.A.

ELM HILL

A Division of
HarperCollins Christian Publishing

www.elmhillbooks.com

© 2020 Rev. Jopie Rattu, Ph.D.; Sridadi Atiyanto, Ph.D.;
Yunus Ciptawilangga, M.B.A.

The Rapture
Part II

Fulfillment of: The Signs in The Sky,
The Festivals in Summer, and The Parables of The End Times

All rights reserved. No portion of this book may be reproduced, stored in a retrieval system, or transmitted in any form or by any means—electronic, mechanical, photocopy, recording, scanning, or other—except for brief quotations in critical reviews or articles, without the prior written permission of the publisher.

Published in Nashville, Tennessee, by Elm Hill, an imprint of Thomas Nelson. Elm Hill and Thomas Nelson are registered trademarks of HarperCollins Christian Publishing, Inc.

Elm Hill titles may be purchased in bulk for educational, business, fund-raising, or sales promotional use. For information, please e-mail SpecialMarkets@ ThomasNelson.com.

Scripture quotations marked KJV are from the King James Version. Public domain.

Scripture quotations marked NIV are from the Holy Bible, New International Version’, NIV’. Copyright © 1973, 1978, 1984, 2011 by Biblica, Inc.’ Used by permission of Zondervan. All rights reserved worldwide. www.Zondervan.com. The “NIV” and “New International Version” are trademarks registered in the United States Patent and Trademark Office by Biblica, Inc.’

Library of Congress Cataloging-in-Publication Data

Library of Congress Control Number: 2019920797

ISBN 978-1-400330393 (Paperback)
ISBN 978-1-400330409 (eBook)

FOREWORD

The main theme of this book is "Rapture," with subthemes "Fulfillment of the Signs in the Sky, Fulfillment of the Festivals in Summer, and Fulfillment of the Parable of the End Times." The main theme is very closely related with the subthemes because the subthemes presented very strong facts that seem to lead are or conical to the main theme, namely, the fact that the rapture is expected to occur at the time as set out in the subthemes.

This second part of the book explains about the signs of heaven that are related to the second coming of the Lord Jesus.

The first coming of the Lord Jesus is marked by a sign in the sky in the form of a star in the east, and it is this star that guides the wise men so that they can meet the Lord Jesus as explained in Matthew 2:2,9:

> *Saying, Where is he that is born King of the Jews? for we have seen his **star in the east**, and are come to worship him.*
>
> *When they had heard the king, they departed; and, lo, **the star**, which they saw **in the east**, went before them, till it came and stood over where the young child was.*
>
> (Mt 2:2, 9)

God also gave signs in the sky relating to the second coming of the Lord Jesus as recorded in the following:

> ***The sun shall be turned into darkness, and the moon into blood***, *before that great and notable day of the Lord come.*

(ACTS 2:20)

From 2014 to 2019, there were sixteen sky signs referred to the verse, in the form of nine solar eclipses and seven total lunar eclipses (moons like blood), all of which **occur right** on the feast days of the people of Israel or **the days that we interpret related to end-time events**.

In addition, the book also explains the Israelite festivals and their meanings and prophecies. The Israelites have seven main feasts which are divided into two, namely, the festivals of rainy season and the festival of summer. The three festivals of the rainy season were fulfilled at the time of the first coming of the Lord Jesus. The Lord Jesus died on the feast of Passover as the Lamb of God sacrificed for the salvation of mankind. He rose on the Feast of the Firstfruits, as the first to rise from the dead. And finally the Holy Spirit was poured out on the day of Pentecost, where previously the Word of God was engraved on tablets of stone, now carved into the hearts of men.

The four summer festivals in the form of the Feast of the Trumpet, the Day of Atonement, the Feast of Tabernacles, and the day of Hanukkah have not yet been fulfilled. Many theologians believe that the holidays will be fulfilled in connection with the second coming of the Lord Jesus.

Surprisingly, when we interpreted end-time events based on data of solar eclipses and total lunar eclipses, Israel's feasts, and Bible verses, it turns out that our interpretation of the end-time events **occurred precisely** in the days the summer feast is in accordance with the prophecies of these feast days so that if this really happens, then the second coming of the Lord Jesus will be the fulfillment of the Israel's summer festivals!

Signs of heaven that are so real that God gave us would spur us to better prepare ourselves to welcome His coming.

In the first part of the book, the authors present very basic things that should be known by Christians, namely, things relating to the end times which include the following:

- Signs and marks 666 which must not be accepted by Christians
- The importance of knowing the Last World Ruler
- Characteristics of the four prominent end times figures: "who are they"
- Rapture: what and when
- The difference between the tribulation period and God's wrath period
- Tribulation period: when it starts and ends
- The events that occurred related to the opening of each seal of the seven seals in the Book of Revelation
- Emergence and duties of "two witnesses of God"
- Christian preparations and attitudes in the end times

In addition, at the end of this book, the *estimated* "The Book of Revelation in a New Structure" is included.

Many Christians have difficulty understanding the contents of the Book of Revelation. This happened, for one thing, because the contents and events in the Book of Revelation were not sequential from beginning to end; there are several events that were repeated in other sections. Why do some repetitions occur? Because the Apostle John wrote the Book of Revelation from two visions, where some of the two visions are related to the same things. For example, seven trumpets are the same as seven vials of the wrath, the appointment of 144,000 people from the tribes of the descendants of Israel is explained twice (Rev 7:4 and Rev 14:1), and the people in heaven is also explained twice (Rev 7:13–14 and Rev 15:2). If all the same events are put together so that the contents of the Book of Revelation are sequential in time from beginning to end, then the Book of Revelation becomes easy to understand and even the meaning of the seven seals is easier to understand, without needing to be interpreted, because the meaning of the first to the third seal is found in another chapter of the Book of Revelation.

But we have this treasure in earthen vessels, that the excellency of the power may be of God, and not of us.

(2 Co 4:7)

Soli Deo Gloria,
Authors

CHAPTER 1

INTRODUCTION

Several years lately many servants of God have made interpretations of the end times, including the three of us (Rev. Jopie Rattu, PhD, Mr. Sridadi Atiyanto, PhD, and Yunus Ciptawilangga, MBA). We also wrote books on the end times, as well as interpretations and commentaries on it.

The interpretations which say that today we are in the end times, among others, are marked by the legalization of a law of health insurance known as **Obamacare** on March 23, 2010. The official name of Obamacare is "Patient Protection and Affordable Care Act" or better known as "Health Care Bill HR 3200." Obamacare is linked with the end of time because the law requires each participant to have a **chip implanted** in her/his body.

The subject about the end times heightened when **Pastor Mark Biltz** found out the phenomenon of the moon became bloodred, which later was called the **blood moon** and was believed to be one of the signs of the end times. Moreover it was later discovered that the blood moon in the year 2014–2015 occurred four times and **all four took place during the Israelite festivals**, which was at the Feast of

Passover and the Feast of Tabernacles in 2014 and also in the year 2015, at the Feast of Passover and the Feast of Tabernacles. On further studies and observations, it turned out that there occurred not only four blood moons or tetrad blood moon, but also **two solar eclipses**, namely, a total solar eclipse on the Israelite New Year and another one at the Feast of Trumpets.

2014		2015				
Apr - 15	Oct - 08	Mar - 20	Apr - 04	Sep - 13	Sep - 23	Sep - 28
		Sabbatical Year				
Nissan 14	Tishri 15	Nissan 1	Nissan 14	Tishri 1	Tishri 10	Tishri 15
Passover	Tabernacles	1st Cal. Year	Passover	Trumpets	Yom Kippur	Tabernacles

Furthermore, Mark Biltz's discovery was strengthened by the discovery of Paul Grevas, a statistician, who discovered that in addition to the tetrad blood moon that occurred in 2014–2015, there were also eclipses that occurred both before and after the tetrad blood moon that formed the formation of perfect symmetry when calculated from the centerlines of the eclipses. The formation of eclipses is so perfect it is certainly something that is very surprising. That is why Paul Grevas declared these perfect symmetrical eclipses as **God's Perfect Sign**.

Introduction

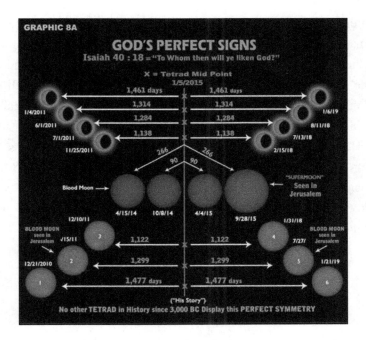

In accordance with Acts 2:20, *"The sun shall be turned into darkness, and the moon into blood, before that great and notable day of the Lord come,"* many servants of God believe that those signs in the sky are the intended marks mentioned in that verse so that many people watch for what would happen in the years connected with the appearance of the blood moons.

But unfortunately, when people waited for the appearance of the first blood moon on April 15, 2014, apparently nothing happened. Even at the appearance of the other eclipses, nothing happened. Similarly, when the last blood moon occurred on September 28, 2015, which could be seen in Jerusalem, there was no significant incident as well. Hence, since then almost every servant of God who has written or discussed about the signs in the sky related to the end of time felt "disheartened" and became silent, including us. Why so? Because nothing happened—any significant or extraordinary event that we believed would happen did not happen at all. So after that, we began to search everywhere throughout the Internet to know the response of the other servants of God who made interpretations and comments on the end times. Almost all who had made interpretations on the end times apologized, and so did we, whereas the interpretations seemed so convincing.

However, early in last August 2016, we got back those signs with a very surprising understanding that the eclipses of years 2018 **have the same interval of days** with the ones in 2015, especially when reckoned from the calendar year beginning on the first day of Nisan and the other one beginning on the fifteenth day of Shevat.

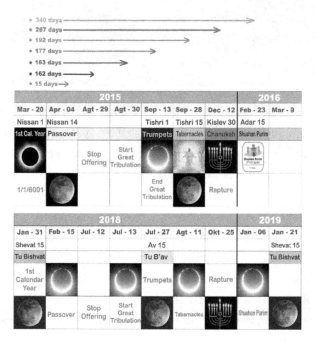

The eclipses in 2015 compared with the eclipses in 2018

INTRODUCTION

In addition, of the five eclipses that occurred in 2018, four eclipses occurred on the feast days of the Israelites as happened in 2015, and **one eclipse occurred on the day that we interpreted would be the beginning of great tribulation**.

Furthermore, in 2019 there were four eclipses in which one eclipse occurred on the Jewish feast day as happened in 2018, one eclipse occurred on the feast of Purim, and **two eclipses occurred on the days that we interpreted as events related to the end times, namely, the day of the cessation of daily sacrifices and the last day of great tribulation in Jerusalem**.

The occurrence of the eclipses in 2018 and 2019 **exactly** on the days that we interpreted will occur in the events of the end times strengthens our belief that it is very likely that the end times will occur according to what we interpret.

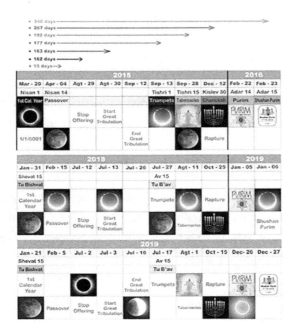

Yet before we discuss about the subject, let's go back for a moment.

The Bible records many signs of the end times, both those conveyed by the Lord Jesus and by the Apostles and prophets.

Earthquakes

The Lord Jesus explained to His disciples that by the end times, there will be earthquakes in various places.

*For nation shall rise against nation, and kingdom against kingdom: and there shall be **earthquakes in divers places**, and there shall be famines and troubles: these are the beginnings of sorrows.*

(MARK 13:8)

Living in Indonesia we may already feel it; at least once a week, an earthquake occurs and sometimes even less than a week. However, the earthquakes occur not only in Indonesia, but in the world at large; even terrible earthquakes have occurred in Italy, Ecuador, China, Taiwan, and other countries. Some time ago the Kyushu Island in Japan was hit by earthquakes even as many as 600 times within five days.

Eating and Drinking

Furthermore the Lord Jesus explained that before the end times, people will not only eat and drink because of the numerous vendors selling all kinds of food and drinks, but they even eat and drink at inappropriate places or spots.

INTRODUCTION

*For as in the days that were before the flood they were **eating and drinking**, marrying and giving in marriage, until the day that Noe entered into the ark.*

(MT 24:38)

Nowadays we see food and drinks vendors increase. Along the ways and even in the corners, we can find food and drinks being sold not only in Indonesia but in almost all countries in the world. In Waikiki of Hawaii, hotel lobbies are turned into restaurants or cafés so that the lobbies become small. Then *food channels* grow rapidly in number. There are Love Eating, Food Crazy, Culinary, Chef Traveller, Iron Chef, Come Dine with Me, Hell's Kitchen, Asian Food Channel, and many other TV channels, which discuss food.

Nowadays many celebrity chefs pop up. The parents of one of the authors of this book opened a restaurant when he was nine years old, and there was no cook or chef who became a celebrity then. Basically, a cook can be associated with a mechanic. No mechanic has become a celebrity. But nowadays a cook can become a celebrity and is welcomed everywhere. To us this is something strange that has never happened before.

The same with restaurants. Today running a restaurant or a café is considered prestigious. There is a sense of pride when someone plunges into the business of owning a café or restaurant. As it was mentioned earlier, one of the authors of this book comes from a family who owned a restaurant. In the days of his father, people in this business were categorized as lacking the financial capital. Those who owned an adequate capital would try textile business, attempt as wholesalers or distributors, make efforts in industrial projects, and do other businesses, not running a restaurant. Even in the year 1990s, when he began to be more serious in this restaurant business, it was regarded a business for people of minimum capital. Yet nowadays the tycoons, celebrities, and even famous artists occupy themselves in restaurant business and they are very proud.

As we studied about the end times, we saw that the signs of the end times were always uncommon signs, likewise regarding eating and drinking. We saw that eating and drinking in the verse above were not only concerning the number of food and beverage vendors, but also the rampant phenomena of **eating and drinking during the worship service in the church**. The author is very sad to witness these phenomena. Are not these actions a demonstration of **disrespecting or dishonoring God**? Why? The simplest explanation is this: When we pay a visit to someone's home and we act improperly there, what does it mean? Yes, it means that we are insulting the host! Likewise, if we act improperly during the worship service in the church, which is the house of God, then actually we are insulting God as the owner or the host there.

We all have been going to church for years, and as far as we can remember, we never saw people eating and drinking in the church, let alone saw pastors drinking coffee and placing the tumbler on the pulpit while preaching as we sometimes see these days.

Marrying and Giving in Marriage

The Lord Jesus also explained that in the end times, people would be found marrying and giving in marriage inappropriately.

*For as in the days that were before the flood they were eating and drinking, **marrying and giving in marriage**, until the day that Noe entered into the ark.*

(Mt 24:38)

INTRODUCTION

In the same manner as the explanation or description above, marrying and giving in marriage mentioned in the preceding verse is certainly not just marrying and giving in marriage as is customary. One of them could be among LGBT which is flaring up lately. But there is another phenomenon, namely, the diffusion and increase of an adult marrying a kid. This is no pedophile, since pedophiles rape children. This is a real marriage but with a child, and there are even instances of an adult man marrying a girl of ten years old.

Kompas.com October 11, 2016, shared the news that every seven seconds, at least one little girl under fifteen years of age is married off to an older man in some countries in the world.

UNICEF, the United Nations International Children's Emergency Fund, estimated the number of women who get married while still underage would increase from 700 million today to about 950 million in 2030.

CHAPTER 2

FULFILLMENT OF THE
SIGNS IN THE SKY

As has been mentioned in Chapter 1, Pastor Mark Biltz found out the phenomenon of the moon became bloodred, which later was called **the blood moon** and was believed to be one of the signs of the end times. Moreover it was later discovered that in the year 2014–2015, there were four blood moons and two solar eclipses occurred and **all six took place during the Israelite festivals**.

2014		2015				
Apr - 15	Oct - 08	Mar - 20	Apr - 04	Sep - 13	Sep - 23	Sep - 28
Sabbatical Year						
Nissan 14	Tishri 15	Nissan 1	Nissan 14	Tishri 1	Tishri 10	Tishri 15
Passover	Tabernacles	1st Cal. Year	Passover	Trumpets	Yom Kippur	Tabernacles

God's Perfect Signs in the Sky

A Greek statistician named Paul Grevas has studied the "Biblical Blood Moon Tetrad," which is four total lunar eclipses that occur consecutively in the first year; two total lunar eclipses are to happen on the day of the Passover and at the Feast of Tabernacles and then similar events happen in the following year, the one as occurred in 2014–2015.

In his investigation, Paul Grevas used documents from NASA where data of the lunar and solar eclipses in the span of 6,000 years, from 3000 BC till 3000 AD, are kept safe.

Statistically, the probability that the Biblical Blood Moon Tetrad would occur is one in $1.85 \times (10)^{139}$ or 1.85 x 1 with 139 zeros. For comparison, 1 million is $(10)^6 = 1,000,000$; 1 billion is $(10)^9 = 1,000,000,000$; and 1 trillion is $(10)^{12} = 1,000,000,000,000$. Now, if the probability of the Biblical Blood Moon Tetrad to occur is one in $1.85 \times (10)^{139}$, the possibility of this to happen is considered very very small and can be ignored. So when the Biblical Blood Moon Tetrad happens, that certainly can not happen by pure chance.

The assessment of this probability does not include the possibility of adding to the Biblical Blood Moon Tetrad the solar eclipse that may happen on other feast days of the Israelites. As happened during 2014–2015, besides the Biblical Blood Moon Tetrad, there were also two solar eclipses on other feast days of the Israelites.

Paul Grevas investigated that the next Biblical Blood Moon Tetrad would happen again during 2582–2583 or about 565 years from now.

When we look at the condition of the world today:

- The threat of nuclear weapon increases since more and more countries own it.
- Free sex, marriage between same sex, and abortion increase.
- Many people become even more greedy and immoral.

- The evil intensifies and there is loss of love toward our fellow man.

Consequently, it is unlikely that the Lord Jesus will come 565 years from now.

Since 3,000 years before Christ until today, the Biblical Blood Moon Tetrad had occurred eight times. And very interestingly, every time it occurred, it was always connected with some big event regarding the Israel.

An Extraordinary Natural Phenomenon

The first Biblical Blood Moon Tetrad was preceded by an extraordinary natural phenomenon which occurred at the time of the crucifixion of the Lord Jesus.

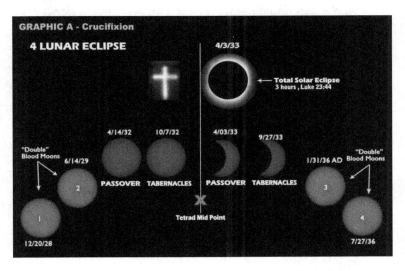

Graphic A: There were four lunar eclipses in the year 32 and 33 AD—two total lunar eclipses and two partial lunar eclipses. Two other total lunar eclipses occurred before (28–29AD) and another two after (36 AD) those four lunar eclipses. In addition, there was also a total solar eclipse on the day of Passover in the year 33 AD.

THE RAPTURE

These signs in the sky were connected with the crucifixion of the Lord Jesus that occurred on the day of Passover in the year 33 AD.

If we study Graphic A above, we will come up with the following:

- There were two total lunar eclipses in the year 32 AD and two partial lunar eclipses in the year 33 AD.
- In the year 32 AD, the moon looked like blood (blood moon) on the day of Passover and at the Feast of Tabernacles.
- In the year 33 AD, there was a partial lunar eclipse on the day of Passover and another one at the Feast of Tabernacles.
- On April 3, 33 AD, exactly on the day of Passover, a total solar eclipse (total darkness) happened according to Luke 23: 44–45:

  *And it was about the sixth hour, and there was a **darkness over all the earth** until the ninth hour. And the sun was darkened, and the veil of the temple was rent in the midst.*

- Only two total lunar eclipses occurred before and another two after the tetrad lunar eclipses.

FULFILLMENT OF THE SIGNS IN THE SKY

First Biblical Blood Moon Tetrad

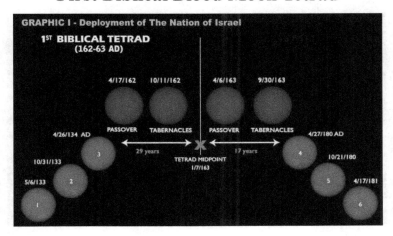

Graphic 1: First Biblical Blood Moon Tetrad during 162–163 AD. There were three total lunar eclipses before and another three after the Biblical Blood Moon Tetrad.

In the year when those signs in the sky occurred, the people of Israel dispersed to the Continent (Europe) because of the persecution by the Roman Emperor Marcus Aurelius Antoninus.

If we study Graphic 1 above, we will come up with the following:

- There were three total lunar eclipses before and another three after the first Biblical Blood Moon Tetrad.
- If we take the midpoint of the Biblical Blood Moon Tetrad which falls on January 7, 163 AD, the interval from the third total lunar eclipse to the midpoint is twenty-nine years, while the interval from the fourth total lunar eclipse to the midpoint is seventeen years.

THE RAPTURE

Second Biblical Blood Moon Tetrad

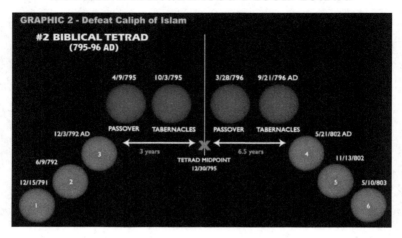

Graphic 2: Second Biblical Blood Moon Tetrad during 795–796 AD. There were three total lunar eclipses before and three others thereafter.

In the year when those signs in the sky occurred, the caliph of Islam made war to take possession over the European countries but was defeated by King Charlemagne. In this battle millions of Christians and Jews were killed.

If we study Graphic 2 above, we will come up with the following:

- There were three total lunar eclipses before and another three after the second Biblical Blood Moon Tetrad.
- If we take the midpoint of the Biblical Blood Moon Tetrad which falls on December 30, 795 AD, the interval from the third total lunar eclipse to the midpoint is three years, while the interval from the fourth total lunar eclipse to the midpoint is six and a half years.

FULFILLMENT OF THE SIGNS IN THE SKY

Third Biblical Blood Moon Tetrad

Graphic 3: The third Biblical Blood Moon Tetrad during 842–843 AD.
There were three total lunar eclipses before and another three thereafter.
There were also four partial solar eclipses before and another four thereafter.

At the time those signs in the sky occurred, the Roman Empire collapsed as the Moslem country succeeded in taking control of the Byzantine (Turkey), and in that warfare, millions of Christians and Jews were killed.

If we study Graphic 3 above, we will come up with the following:

- There were three total lunar eclipses before and another three after the third Biblical Blood Moon Tetrad.
- There were four partial solar eclipses before and another four after the third Biblical Blood Moon Tetrad.
- If we take the midpoint of the Biblical Blood Moon Tetrad which falls on December 20, 842 AD, the interval from the

17

fourth partial solar eclipse to the midpoint is three years, while the interval from the fifth partial solar eclipse to the midpoint is six years.

Fourth Biblical Blood Moon Tetrad

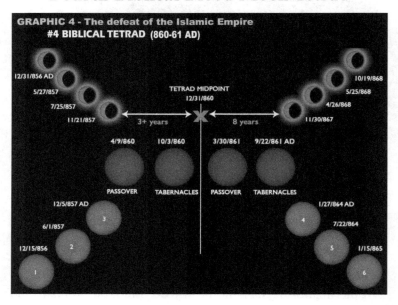

Graphic 4: The fourth Biblical Blood Moon Tetrad during 860–861 AD. There were three total lunar eclipses before and another three thereafter. There were also four partial solar eclipses before and another four thereafter.

At the time those signs in the sky occurred, the Moslem Empire tried to gain dominion over the world but was defeated by the European countries. In the event millions of Christians and Jews were killed.

If we study Graphic 4 above, we will come up with the following:

- There were three total lunar eclipses before and another three after the fourth Biblical Blood Moon Tetrad.

FULFILLMENT OF THE SIGNS IN THE SKY

- There were four partial solar eclipses before and another four after the fourth Biblical Blood Moon Tetrad.
- If we take the midpoint of the Biblical Blood Moon Tetrad which falls on December 31, 860 AD, the interval from the fourth partial solar eclipse to the midpoint is three years, while the interval from the fifth partial solar eclipse to the midpoint is eight years.

Fifth Biblical Blood Moon Tetrad

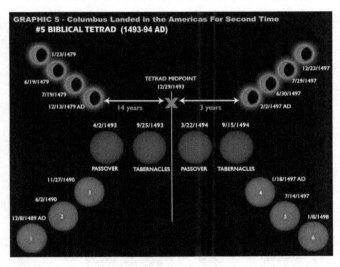

Graphic 5: Fifth Biblical Blood Moon Tetrad during 1493–1494. There were three total lunar eclipses before the Biblical Blood Moon Tetrad and another three thereafter. There were also four partial solar eclipses before and another four thereafter.

At the time those signs in the sky occurred, Columbus anchored at the American continent for the second time, and that was the beginning of the colonization of the American continent.

If we study Graphic 5 above, we will come up with the following:

THE RAPTURE

- There were three total lunar eclipses before and another three after the fifth Biblical Blood Moon Tetrad.
- There were four partial solar eclipses before and another four after the fifth Biblical Blood Moon Tetrad.
- If we take the midpoint of the Biblical Blood Moon Tetrad which falls on December 29, 1493 AD, the interval from the fourth partial solar eclipse to the midpoint is fourteen years, while the interval from the fifth partial solar eclipse to the midpoint is three years.

Sixth Biblical Blood Moon Tetrad

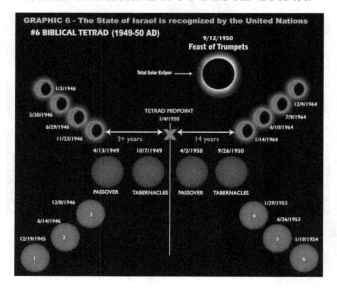

Graphic 6: Sixth Biblical Blood Moon Tetrad during 1949–1950.
There were three total lunar eclipses before and another three thereafter.
There were also four partial solar eclipses before and another four thereafter.
There was also a total solar eclipse at the Feast of Trumpets.

20

FULFILLMENT OF THE SIGNS IN THE SKY

At the time those signs in the sky occurred, the independence of the State of Israel gained recognition from the United Nations.

If we study Graphic 6 above, we will come up with the following:

- There were three total lunar eclipses before and another three after the sixth Biblical Blood Moon Tetrad.
- There were four partial solar eclipses before and another four after the sixth Biblical Blood Moon Tetrad.
- A total solar eclipse occurred at the Feast of Trumpets.
- If we take the midpoint of the Biblical Blood Moon Tetrad which falls on January 4, 1950 AD, the interval from the fourth partial solar eclipse to the midpoint is three years, while the interval from the fifth partial solar eclipse to the midpoint is fourteen years.

Seventh Biblical Blood Moon Tetrad

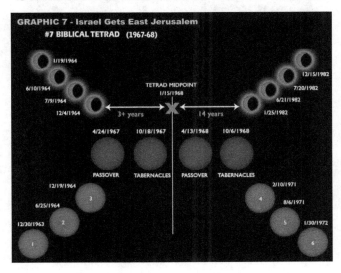

Graphic 7: Seventh Biblical Blood Moon Tetrad during 1967–1968.
There were three total lunar eclipses before and another three thereafter.
There were also four partial solar eclipses before and another four thereafter.

21

THE RAPTURE

At the time those signs in the sky occurred, the Israelites gained dominion over East Jerusalem as the result of the six-day war.

If we study Graphic 7 above, we will come up with the following:

- There were three total lunar eclipses before and another three after the seventh Biblical Blood Moon Tetrad.
- There were four partial solar eclipses before and another four after the seventh Biblical Blood Moon Tetrad.
- If we take the midpoint of the Biblical Blood Moon Tetrad which falls on January 4, 1950, the interval from the fourth partial solar eclipse to the midpoint is three years, while the interval from the fifth partial solar eclipse to the midpoint is fourteen years.

The Eighth Biblical Blood Moon Tetrad

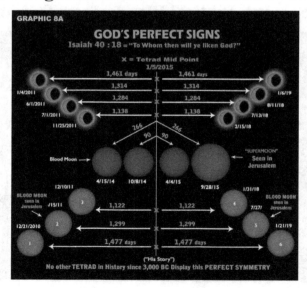

Graphic 8A: Eighth Biblical Blood Moon Tetrad during 2014–2015. There were three total lunar eclipses before and there will be another three thereafter. There were also four partial solar eclipses before and there will be another four thereafter.

22

FULFILLMENT OF THE SIGNS IN THE SKY

If we study Graphic 8A above, we will come up with the following:

- If we take the midpoint of the Biblical Blood Moon Tetrad which will falls on January 5, 2015, the interval from the first total lunar eclipse to the midpoint is **exactly the same as** from the fourth total lunar eclipse to the midpoint (266 days), also from the second or the third lunar eclipse to the midpoint (90 days). There is no difference at all, not even one day.
- Similarly, the three total lunar eclipses that occurred before that Biblical Blood Moon Tetrad each had the same interval as the coming one paired with it when calculated from the day of its occurrence to the midpoint. (Check the first and the sixth, the second and the fifth, and the third and the fourth.)
- This is also true with the four partial solar eclipses that occurred before the Biblical Blood Moon Tetrad. Each had the same interval as the expected one paired with it when calculated from the day of its occurrence to the midpoint.
- The second total lunar eclipse on June 15, 2011, was seen in Jerusalem as well as the coming one paired with it, namely, the fifth total lunar eclipse, which would be seen there on July 27, 2018.
- The last blood moon in the year 2015 that would happen at the Feast of Tabernacles is to become a supermoon. It would look larger and could be seen in Jerusalem.

All lunar and the solar eclipses, either total or partial, which are related to the Biblical Blood Moon Tetrad during 2014–2015 are shown below:

THE RAPTURE

Note:

There were three total solar eclipses that occurred before the total lunar eclipse (blood moon) on December 21, 2010. All three of them were seen on the first day of Av (the fifth month of the Israelite calendar), namely:

- Total solar eclipse on the first day of Av, 2008
- Total solar eclipse on the first day of Av, 2009
- Total solar eclipse on the first day of Av, 2010

If we observe how the solar eclipses and the total lunar eclipses during 2014–2015 and also other eclipses before or thereafter occurred in such orderly and symmetrical sequence, then surely they could not happen accidentally. Why? Because unlike a shooting star or a falling star that can happen at any time, a solar eclipse or a lunar eclipse occurs not haphazardly but following the ***definite* natural law and order** based on the rotation of the sun, moon, and earth. That's why NASA scientists and experts can compute correctly when an eclipse is to happen because the rotations of the three celestial bodies in the solar system are definite. Accordingly, the Israelite festivals are definite too following the Jewish calendar, where the date of each feast day is fixed. Hence the Biblical

Blood Moon Tetrad during 2014–2015 and the accompanying eclipses definitely happened because a tremendous power controls them. Since statistically the probability that a Biblical Blood Moon Tetrad may occur is 1 in 1.85 x $(10)^{139}$, we can imagine how small the chance is for the symmetrical eclipses to happen, like those accompanying the Biblical Blood Moon Tetrad during 2014–2015. We are sure that no one, however genius he might be, is capable of doing such an amazing thing, even if only to compute, moreover to set up for it to happen exactly as the Biblical Blood Moon Tetrad during 2014–2015.

Indeed it is obviously a sign from God to make us aware of at least three things:

1. There will be some phenomenal events related to those signs in the sky.
2. God demonstrated His power to mankind so that we would be aware and understand that there is no one like the LORD God.

To whom then will ye liken God? Or what likeness will ye compare unto him?

(ISAIAH 40:18, KJV)

or

To whom, then, will you compare God? Or what image will you compare him to?

(NIV)

3. God wants to convince His children of all His promises.

(Source: http://bloodmoonscoming.com)

CHAPTER 3

FULFILLMENT OF THE SUMMER FESTIVALS

The Birth of the Lord Jesus

When we study the birth of the Lord Jesus into this world, it was in accordance with the prophesy over 700 years ago in the Book of Micah:

> *But you, **Bethlehem Ephrathah**, though you are small among the clans of Judah, out of you will come for me **one who will be ruler over Israel**, whose origins are from of old, from ancient times.*

> (MIC 5:2)

So the question is, at the time when the Lord Jesus was born into the world, was there anyone who knew that it was a very special event?

The answer is yes, there were. The Magi mentioned in Matthew 2 were described as follows:

THE RAPTURE

Now when Jesus was born in Bethlehem of Judaea in the days of Herod the king, behold, there came wise men from the east to Jerusalem,

*Saying, Where is he that is born King of the Jews? for we have seen **his star in the east**, and are come to worship him.*

(MT 2:1–2)

How come that the wise men knew about it? For they saw His star in the sky. And when we read further, the star was not only to mark that a King or the Messiah was born, but it also led the wise men to the place where the infant Jesus was.

When they had heard the king, they departed; and, lo, the star, which they saw in the east, went before them, till it came and stood over where the young child was.

(MT 2:9)

Since the time of the first coming of the Lord Jesus—His birth as a human being on earth—was recognized by some people, would the time of His second coming also be known?

In the Bible we read that when God destroyed the human population in Noah's day by the flood, God apparently told Noah in advance about the time He would send rain upon the earth and also how long the rain would pour down, as it was written:

*For yet **seven days**, and I will cause it to rain upon the earth **forty days and forty nights**; and every living substance that I have made will I destroy from off the face of the earth.*

(GENESIS 7:4)

28

FULFILLMENT OF THE SUMMER FESTIVALS

Even so, before the Lord destroyed Sodom and Gomorrah, He revealed in advance to Abraham and Lot about the destruction that would happen.

> *And the LORD said, Because the cry of **Sodom and Gomorrah** is great, and because their sin is very grievous.*
>
> (GENESIS 18:20)

> *And when the morning arose, then the angels hastened **Lot**, saying, Arise, take thy wife, and thy two daughters, which are here; lest thou be consumed in the iniquity of the city.*
>
> (GENESIS 19:15)

The Coming of the Lord Jesus Is Like a Thief

While there was a prior notice about the time of the flood to Noah and the destruction of Sodom and Gomorrah to Abraham and Lot, could it be that the second coming of the Lord Jesus also be notified and the signs given in advance? Remember, is it not written in the Bible that the Lord Jesus will come like a thief in the night?

> *But of the times and the seasons, brethren, ye have no need that I write unto you.*
>
> *For yourselves know perfectly that the day of the Lord so cometh as **a thief in the night**.*
>
> (1 THESSALONIANS 5:1–2)

Yes, it is true that the Lord Jesus will come like a thief in the night. But for whom? Now, if we read the verses further, we will realize then that:

THE RAPTURE

For when they shall say, Peace and safety; then sudden destruction cometh upon them, as travail upon a woman with child; and they shall not escape.

*But ye, brethren, **are not in darkness, that that day should overtake you as a thief.***

(1 THESSALONIANS 5:3–4)

Verse 4 above explains clearly that we are not to live in darkness. So when the Lord Jesus will come like a thief, it has the connotation that as children of light, we will be told exactly when it is going to happen. As children of light, we will know when the day of the coming of the Lord Jesus will be, due to the reasons described in verse 5:

Ye are all the children of light, and the children of the day*: we are not of the night, nor of darkness.*

(1 THESSALONIANS 5:5)

To the sons of the night or sons of the darkness, the coming of the Lord Jesus will be like a thief in the night.

Therefore, we are admonished not to fall asleep nor get drunk like the sons of the night:

*Therefore **let us not sleep, as do others; but let us watch and be sober**.*

For they that sleep sleep in the night; and they that be drunken are drunken in the night.

But let us, who are of the day, be sober, putting on the breastplate of faith and love; and for an helmet, the hope of salvation.

1 THESSALONIANS 5:6–8

FULFILLMENT OF THE SUMMER FESTIVALS

As the sons of the day, we must be:

- **Alert**
  Since the time of the Lord Jesus' coming is as definite as the coming of dawn, and imminent, we therefore should be able to control ourselves and be clearminded so that we can pray. We must also guard ourselves against all the wiles of the devil.

  But the end of all things is at hand: be ye therefore sober, and watch unto prayer.

  (1 PETER 4:7)

  Be sober, be vigilant; because your adversary the devil, as a roaring lion, walketh about, seeking whom he may devour.

  (1 PETER 5:8)

- **Putting on faith and love as a breastplate**
  Put on faith and love as the armor of God to take our stand against the devil's schemes.

  Put on the whole armour of God, that ye may be able to stand against the wiles of the devil.

  (EPH 6:11)

- **Putting on the hope of salvation as a helmet**
  Protect oneself against all the wiles of the devil with the assurance of our salvation through God's Word.

THE RAPTURE

And take the helmet of salvation, and the sword of the Spirit, which is the word of God.

(EPH 6:17)

Furthermore the Bible also recorded that God's plans were always revealed to His children:

- *Surely the Lord GOD will do nothing, but he revealeth his secret unto his servants the prophets.* (Amos 3:7)
- *Henceforth I call you not servants; for the servant knoweth not what his lord doeth: but I have called you friends; for all things that I have heard of my Father I have made known unto you.* (Jn. 15:15)
- *But God hath revealed them unto us by his Spirit: for the Spirit searcheth all things, yea, the deep things of God.* (1 Co 2:10)

Even though many verses declare that God's children as children of light will know about the time of the Lord Jesus' coming, we are often confused by what is stated in Matthew 24:36:

But of that day and hour knoweth no man, no, not the angels of heaven, **but my Father only**.

(KJV)

Or: *No one knows about that day or hour, not even the angels in heaven, nor the Son, but **only** the Father.*

(NIV)

FULFILLMENT OF THE SUMMER FESTIVALS

The verse above seems to proclaim that the time of the Lord Jesus' coming will not be known to anyone, nor Jesus himself—only known by the Father.

To understand the meaning of that verse more clearly, let's study it in its original language:

Περὶ δὲ τῆς ἡμέρας ἐκείνης καὶ ὥρας οὐδεὶς οἶδεν, οὐδὲ οἱ ἄγγελοι τῶν οὐρανῶν, **εἰ μὴ** ὁ πατὴρ μου μόνος.

(Mat 24:36)

Matthew 24:36

"But of that day and hour knoweth no man, no, not the angels of heaven, but my Father only."

3588 [e]	τῶν tōn	of the	Art-GMP
3772 [e]	οὐρανῶν ouranōn	heavens,	N-GMP
3761 [e]	οὐδὲ oude	nor	Conj
3588 [e]	ὁ ho	the	Art-NMS
5207 [e]	Υἱός, Huios	Son,	N-NMS
1487 [e]	εἰ ei	if	Conj
3361 [e]	μὴ mē	not	Adv
3588 [e]	ὁ ho	the	Art-NMS
3962 [e]	Πατήρ Patēr	Father	N-NMS
3441 [e]	μόνος. monos	only.	Adj-NMS

From the above data, the word "only" in this verse comes from the word "ei me" which means "if not," so Matthew 24:36 can be translated this way:

*No one knows about that day or hour, not even the angels in heaven, nor the Son, **if not** the Father.*

(Mt 24:36)

33

It means that if the Lord Jesus were not the Father, then Jesus would not know, but John 10:30, 14:9 explicitly confirms that:

I and my Father are one.

...he that hath seen me hath seen the Father.

So now it is clear that the Lord Jesus knew the time of His second coming, and He had announced it while still living on earth and testified to John about it in the Book of Revelation as written below:

The revelation of Jesus Christ, which God gave him to show his servants what must soon take place. *He made it known by sending his angel to his servant John, who testifies to everything he saw—that is, the word of God and* **the testimony of Jesus Christ.**

(REVELATION 1:1–2)

Thus the conclusion is that we are told about His second coming, that is why as children of light, we have to watch for the signs of the times and observe the prophecies told clearly through the Word of God, for example, the prophetic festive days that God commanded His chosen people, the Israelites, to celebrate.

Festivals of the Israelites

When God created the universe, besides the heavens and the earth, God also created other celestial objects as signs, written in the verses below:

FULFILLMENT OF THE SUMMER FESTIVALS

*And God said, Let there be lights in the firmament of the heaven to **divide the day from the night**; and let them **be for signs**, and **for seasons**, and **for days**, and **years**:*

And let them be for lights in the firmament of the heaven to give light upon the earth: and it was so.

And God made two great lights; the greater light to rule the day, and the lesser light to rule the night: he made the stars also.

(GENESIS 1:14–16)

Verse 16 describes that the larger object of light is the sun to govern the day and the smaller is the moon to rule the night. Verse 14 explains that the objects of light in the sky, the sun and the moon, serve as:

- Signs to separate the day from the night
- Signs to mark seasons
- Signs to mark days and years

What is the meaning of "signs to mark **seasons**"?

Studies of the original language show that the word translated seasons derives from the word "mow`ed (mo-ade')" which could mean *appointed (sign, time), (place of, solemn) assembly, congregation, **(set, solemn) feast**, (appointed, due) season, solemn(-ity), synagogue, (set) time (appointed).*

Since the word "mow`ed (mo-ade')" can also mean "(set, solemn) feast" or "a fixed or set festive day, or a great celebration day," now then, the Word can be translated as follows:

35

THE RAPTURE

*And God said: And God said, Let there be lights in the firma-
ment of the heaven to divide the day from the night; and let
them be for signs, and **for the fixed festive day or the great
time/period**, and for days, and years.*

(GENESIS 1:14, KJV)

*Or Let there be lights in the expanse of the sky to separate the
day from the night, and let them serve as signs to mark **the
fixed festive day or the great time/period** and days and years.*

(NIV)

from the night,	הַלָּיְלָה (hal·la·ve·lah;)	3915: night	of uncertain derivation
and let them be for signs	לְאֹתֹת (le·'o·tot)	226: a sign	from avah
and for seasons	וּלְמוֹעֲדִים (u·le·mo·v·'a·dim,)	4150: appointed time, place, or meeting	from yaad
and for days	וּלְיָמִים (u·le·ya·mim)	3117: day	a prim. root
and years;	וְשָׁנִים: (ve·sha·nim.)	8141: a year	from shana

Thus the verse explains that the sun and the moon also can be
signs to mark the fixed festive days or the great celebration days.

The Israelites have several festivals, and seven of them are important national festivals, consisting of three festivals in the rainy season
and four others in summer, namely:

Festivals in the rainy season:

1. The Passover or *Pesack*
2. Celebration Day of *The Firstfruits*
3. Feast of Pentecost or *Savuot*

Festivals in summer:

1. Feast of Trumpets or *Rosh Hashanah*
2. Day of Atonement or *Yom Kippur*
3. Feast of Tabernacles or *Sukkot*
4. Feast of Hanukkah/Feast of Dedication of the Temple

Interestingly, the three Israelite festivals in the rainy season—the Passover, Celebration Day of the Firstfruits, and the Feast of Pentecost—were fulfilled related to the first coming of Jesus Christ by the evidences as follows:

1. The Passover or Pesack

Celebration of the Passover is recorded in these verses:

*The LORD'S Passover begins at twilight on the **fourteenth day of the first month** (fourteenth day of the first month/Nisan).*

(LEVITICUS 23:5)

And the LORD spake unto Moses and Aaron in the land of Egypt, saying,
    This month shall be unto you the beginning of months: it shall be the first month of the year to you.
    *Speak ye unto all the congregation of Israel, saying, In the tenth day of this month they shall take to them every man **a lamb**, according to the house of their fathers, a lamb for an house:*
    And if the household be too little for the lamb, let him and his neighbour next unto his house take it according to the

The Rapture

number of the souls; every man according to his eating shall make your count for the lamb.

Your lamb shall be without blemish, a male of the first year: ye shall take it out from the sheep, or from the goats:

*And ye shall keep it up **until the fourteenth day of the same month**: and the whole assembly of the congregation of Israel **shall kill it in the evening**.*

*And **they shall take of the blood, and strike it on the two side posts and on the upper door post of the houses**, wherein they shall eat it.*

(EXODUS 12:1–7)

*For I will pass through the land of Egypt this night, and **will smite all the firstborn in the land of Egypt, both man and beast**; and against all the gods of Egypt I will execute judgment: I am the LORD.*

*And **the blood shall be to you for a token** upon the houses where ye are: and when I see the blood, **I will pass over you**, and the plague shall not be upon you to destroy you, when I smite the land of Egypt.*

And this day shall be unto you for a memorial; and ye shall keep it a feast to the LORD throughout your generations; ye shall keep it a feast by an ordinance for ever.

(EXODUS 12:12–14)

God commanded the Israelites to celebrate the Passover as a commemoration of **the sacrificed lamb to redeem the firstborn of the Israelites** when God brought the tenth plague on the Egyptians to kill every firstborn in Egypt, from the firstborn of Pharaoh to the firstborn of the slave and also of all the animals.

FULFILLMENT OF THE SUMMER FESTIVALS

The Passover was fulfilled on the day the commemoration was to begin, through the death of the Lord Jesus as **the Lamb of God sacrificed for the redemption of all mankind**:

> *And **it was the preparation of the passover**, and about the sixth hour: and he saith unto the Jews, Behold your King!*
>
> *But they cried out, Away with him, away with him, crucify him. Pilate saith unto them, Shall I crucify your King? The chief priests answered, We have no king but Caesar.*
>
> *Then delivered he him therefore unto them to be crucified. And they took Jesus, and led him away.*
>
> (JOHN 19:14–16)

2. Celebration Day of the Firstfruits

Celebration Day of the Firstfruits is recorded in the Book of Leviticus:

> *Speak unto the children of Israel, and say unto them, When ye be come into the land which I give unto you, and shall reap the harvest thereof, then **ye shall bring a sheaf of the firstfruits of your harvest unto the priest:***
>
> *And he shall wave the sheaf before the LORD, to be accepted for you: **on the morrow after the sabbath** the priest shall wave it (seventeenth day of the first month/Nisan).*
>
> (LEVITICUS 23:10–11)

Celebration Day of the Firstfruits was also completed by the Lord Jesus on His resurrection as the firstfruits of those who were dead, being described in the following verses:

THE RAPTURE

In the end of the sabbath, as it began to dawn toward the first day of the week, came Mary Magdalene and the other Mary to see the sepulchre.

(MT 28:1)

*But now is Christ risen from the dead, and become **the first-fruits of them that slept.***

(1 Co 15:20)

3. Feast of Pentecost or *Savuot*

The Feast of Pentecost is recorded in the following verses:

And ye shall count unto you from the morrow after the sabbath, from the day that ye brought the sheaf of the wave offering; seven sabbaths shall be complete:

*Even unto the morrow after the seventh sabbath shall ye number **fifty days**; and ye shall offer a new meat offering unto the LORD (sixth day of the third month/Shivan).*

(LEVITICUS 23:15–16)

Feast of Pentecost celebrates not only the gathering of harvest but also the commemoration of the Ten Commandments given to Moses on Mount Sinai. And the feast was completed when the Holy Spirit was poured out on the day of Pentecost as described in the following verses:

*And **when the day of Pentecost was fully come**, they were all with one accord in one place.*

FULFILLMENT OF THE SUMMER FESTIVALS

And suddenly there came a sound from heaven as of a rushing mighty wind, and it filled all the house where they were sitting.

And there appeared unto them cloven tongues like as of fire, and it sat upon each of them.

And they were all filled with the Holy Ghost, *and began to speak with other tongues, as the Spirit gave them utterance.*

(ACT 2:1–4)

On the first Pentecost, God wrote His Words on two tablets of stone (called the two tablets of the Testimony) by His own finger.

And he gave unto Moses, when he had made an end of communing with him upon mount Sinai, two tables of testimony, **tables of stone, written with the finger of God**.

(EXODUS 31:18)

While on the second Pentecost, the Word of God was written with the Spirit of the living God on tablets of human hearts.

Forasmuch as ye are manifestly declared to be the epistle of Christ ministered by us, written not with ink, but **with the Spirit of the living God**; *not in tables of stone, but* **in fleshy tables of the heart**.

(2 CO 3:3)

The four other summer festivals of the Israelites, Feast of Trumpets or *Rosh Hashanah*, Day of Atonement or *Yom Kippur*, Feast of Tabernacles or *Sukkot*, and Feast of the Dedication of the Temple or Hanukkah or Chanukah, are not yet fulfilled.

The purpose of celebrating those festivals and the interpretation or assessment of its fulfillment are explained very clearly by Mr. Abram Thio in his book entitled *Secret Revelation book-1* as follows:

1. Feast of Trumpets or Rosh Hashanah

Feast of Trumpets or Feast of Teruah (*Days of Trumpets*) or also known as a secular festive day Rosh Hashanah (*Jewish New Year*). Feast of Trumpets is recorded in Leviticus 23:24:

> *Speak unto the children of Israel, saying,* **In the seventh month, in the first day of the month**, *shall ye have a sabbath,* **a memorial of blowing of trumpets**, *and holy convocation (first day of the seventh month/Tishri).*

Feast of Trumpets lasts from the first day of *Yamim Noraim* (the ten days of repentance) until the Day of Atonement (Yom Kippur/on the tenth day of the month Tishri).

Rosh Hashanah belongs to the forty days of *Teshuvah* (the turnover or the turning back days) in which thirty days were preparation days beginning on the first Elul (the sixth month), one month full and ten days of *Yamim Noraim* to commemorate the event when Moses ascended Mount Sinai again to receive the Ten Commandments for the second time.

For forty days they blew the trumpets to remind themselves to be faithful to God and never worship idols anymore (the golden calf made by Aaron).

FULFILLMENT OF THE SUMMER FESTIVALS

*And he received them at their hand, and fashioned it with a graving tool, after he had made it **a molten calf**: and they said, **These be thy gods**, O Israel, which brought thee up out of the land of Egypt.*

(EXODUS 32:4)

Feast of Trumpets contains the prophecy that at the end times, the Israelites would again face the challenge to choose to worship idols or not, during the persecution in the *Great Tribulation*.

The antichrist would set up an image (idol) of abominations in Jerusalem and force the people of Judea to worship that image of the *holy man*. Those who refuse to worship the idol will be persecuted and even be killed.

*And deceiveth them that dwell on the earth by the means of those miracles which he had power to do in the sight of the beast; saying to them that dwell on the earth, that **they should make an image to the beast**, which had the wound by a sword, and did live.*

*And he had power to give life unto the image of the beast, that the image of the beast should both speak, and **cause that as many as would not worship the image of the beast should be killed**.*

(REVELATION 13:14–15)

On that occasion the Lord Jesus gave an instruction to the people in Judea to flee out of the city to the mountains as soon as they saw the abomination enter the holy city.

43

THE RAPTURE

> *When ye therefore shall **see the abomination of desolation**, spoken of by Daniel the prophet, **stand in the holy place**, (whoso readeth, let him understand).Then let them which be in Judaea flee into the mountains.*
>
> (Mᴛ 24:15–16)

They were cautioned to persevere until the end and not to join the others in worshiping the image of antichrist nor receive the mark of the beast.

2. Day of Atonement (Yom Kippur)

Day of Atonement or Yom Kippur is the most sacred and solemn celebration of an Israelite festival. This feast is on the tenth day of the Feast of Trumpets as the culmination of the "ten days of repentance" or *Yamim Noraim*.

> *Also on **the tenth day of this seventh month** there shall be a day of atonement: it shall be an holy convocation unto you; and ye shall afflict your souls, and offer an offering made by fire unto the LORD.*
>
> *And ye shall do no work in that same day: for it is a day of atonement, to make an atonement for you before the LORD your God.*
>
> *For whatsoever soul it be that shall not be afflicted in that same day, he shall be cut off from among his people.*
>
> *And whatsoever soul it be that doeth any work in that same day, the same soul will I destroy from among his people.*
>
> *Ye shall do no manner of work: it shall be a statute for ever throughout your generations in all your dwellings.*

FULFILLMENT OF THE SUMMER FESTIVALS

It shall be unto you a sabbath of rest, and ye shall afflict your souls: in the ninth day of the month at even, from even unto even, shall ye celebrate your sabbath (tenth day of the seventh month/Tishri).

(LEVITICUS 23:27–32)

Day of Atonement is the last day to gain God's forgiveness. On that day the Israelites are commanded to fast and humble themselves before the Lord. The Israelites celebrate this festive occasion for twenty-five hours, which lasts from a few minutes before the ninth day of Tishri till the tenth day afternoon. Each year the Day of Atonement is the last chance to determine to show the *Teshuvah* whether someone will be blessed or cursed in the next coming year. On this day of feast, the high priest in earlier times was permitted to enter the most holy place once a year to offer sacrifice for the forgiveness of sins of the Israelites.

The Israelites believe that every year during the celebration of the Feast of Trumpets, God will open the **Sefer Ha Chayim (Book of Life)** and write or erase the names of people due to their deeds or their repentance. They believe that during the ten days of repentance (*Yamim Noraim*), the possibility was still given to the people to have their names written in the Book of Life. But as the Day of Atonement (*Yom Kippur*) was about to end when evening came, the Book of Life would be closed, and whatever had been written in the Book of Life that would determine one's fate in the following year.

The Day of Atonement was prophetic to the culminating events of the Great Tribulation, the time of immense affliction or distress:

THE RAPTURE

*And at that time shall Michael stand up, the great prince which standeth for the children of thy people: and there shall be **a time of trouble**, such as never was since there was a nation even to that same time: and at that time thy people shall be delivered, every one that shall be found written in the book.*

(DA 12:1)

Both the Book of Daniel and the Book of Revelation reveal the close relationship between the names written in the Book of Life and the Great Tribulation in antichrist's time. By this, it meant that the Great Tribulation is closely related to the Day of Atonement (Yom Kippur). We are told that the Book of Life does not contain the names of those who adore antichrist and worship his image.

And all that dwell upon the earth shall worship him, whose names are not written in the book of life of the Lamb slain from the foundation of the world.

(REVELATION 13:8)

3. Feast of the Tabernacles (Sukkot)

Feast of Tabernacles is a national celebration in Israel which is a contrast to the previous festivals, a feast celebrated five days after the most solemn day of commemoration, which is on the fifteenth day of the month Tishri. This should be a festive occasion celebrated with joy at the end of "Teshuvah" which is full of concern and anxiety.

*Also in **the fifteenth day of the seventh month**, when ye have gathered in the fruit of the land, ye shall keep a feast unto the*

46

FULFILLMENT OF THE SUMMER FESTIVALS

LORD seven days: on the first day shall be a sabbath, and on the eighth day shall be a sabbath.

⁴⁰ And ye shall take you on the first day the boughs of goodly trees, branches of palm trees, and the boughs of thick trees, and willows of the brook; and ye shall rejoice before the LORD your God seven days.

(LEVITICUS 23:39–40)

Historically, Feast of Tabernacles commemorated the experiences of the Israelites wandering in the wilderness under the shade of God's **tent**, which was the pillar of cloud by day and the pillar of fire by night. During this journey to the promised land, the Israelites were maintained by God's provision, even though they lived in simple temporary huts or tents in the hard and barren desert.

*Yet thou in thy manifold mercies forsookest them not in the wilderness: **the pillar of the cloud** departed not from them by day, to lead them in the way; neither **the pillar of fire** by night, to shew them light, and the way wherein they should go.*

(NEHEMIAH 9:19)

Feast of Tabernacles or *Sukkot* symbolizes the most anticipated event by the believers, **the rapture**, when all those who believe in Christ (the church or the elect) will be taken up to be with Him forever.

The Bible tells us that the incident will take place shortly after the end of the Great Tribulation.

*But in those days, **after that tribulation**, the sun shall be darkened, and the moon shall not give her light,*

47

THE RAPTURE

And the stars of heaven shall fall, and the powers that are in heaven shall be shaken.

And then **shall they see the Son of man coming in the clouds** *with great power and glory.*

And then shall he send his angels, and **shall gather together his elect from the four winds**, *from the uttermost part of the earth to the uttermost part of heaven.*

(MARK 13:24–27)

Feast of Tabernacles is only five days after the ten days of repentance or *Yamim Noraim*.

Chapter 7 of the Book of Revelation records some characteristics of the Feast of Tabernacles pictured by the taking up of the believers to be in heaven.

The first characteristic is seen in the people carrying **palm fronds**, an instruction to be done at every celebration of the Feast of Tabernacles.

And ye shall take you on the first day the boughs of goodly trees, **branches of palm trees**, *and the boughs of thick trees, and willows of the brook; and ye shall rejoice before the LORD your God seven days.*

(LEVITICUS 23:40)

After this I beheld, and, lo, a great multitude, which no man could number, of all nations, and kindreds, and people, and tongues, stood before the throne, and before the Lamb, clothed with white robes, and **palms** *in their hands.*

(REVELATION 7:9)

FULFILLMENT OF THE SUMMER FESTIVALS

Then the Bible also tells that those people **have come out of the Great Tribulation** and have washed their robes in the blood of the Lamb, which means that they are the ones who have been through the period of great distress, but they remain faithful in their faith in the Lord Jesus, the Lamb of God.

*And I said unto him, Sir, thou knowest. And he said to me, These are they which **came out of great tribulation**, and have washed their robes, and made them white in the blood of the Lamb.*

(REVELATION 7:14)

Considering the aspect of time, this symbolizes that they have been through the period of *Teshuvah* and peace (reconciliation) in *Yom Kippur*, which refers to the next festival, the Feast of Tabernacles. Besides, it is also said that for all of them, God will spread His tent to be their shelter or dwelling place, which was a clear characteristic as to the meaning of *Sukkot* or Feast of Tabernacles.

*Therefore are they before the throne of God, and serve him day and night in his temple: and he that sitteth on the throne shall **dwell** among them.*

(REVELATION 7:15)

Feast of Tabernacles is *agriculturally* often called **the Feast of Gathering the Crops**.

*Thou shalt observe the feast of tabernacles seven days, after that thou **hast gathered** in thy corn and thy wine.*

(DEUTERONOMY 16:13)

THE RAPTURE

The rapture is often referred to as the gathering of the elect (the believers):

*And he shall send his angels with a great sound of a trumpet, and they **shall gather** together his elect from the four winds, from one end of heaven to the other.*

(MT 24:31)

4. Hanukkah/Feast of Dedication of the Temple

Hanukkah is a feast to commemorate the reconsecration of the Temple on the twenty-fifth day of Kislev 165 BC by Judas Maccabaeus, three years after the Temple was desecrated by Antiochus IV Epiphanes who presented pig and the sprinkling of pig blood to the altar. This celebration lasts for eight days and is also known as the Festival of Kenisah (Hanukkah/Chanukah) or the Feast of Dedication of the Temple.

The people of Israel celebrate Hanukkah by marching and bringing along sticks decorated with palm leaves, offering sacrifices, and singing accompanied by musical instruments.

Either in their own homes or in the synagogues, they prepare *menorah* (a lampstand with eight branches, four on the left and four on the right side). Each day one lamp will be lit during the eight-day celebration. It is similar to the custom of lighting one candle each Sunday during the Advent (four Sundays before Christmas or Easter). The Feast of Hanukkah usually falls in the month of December so that the celebration often coincides with the celebration of Christmas and is often mistakenly referred to as the "Jewish Christmas."

The Gospel of John records that the Lord Jesus once had joined the Feast of Dedication or Hanukkah at Jerusalem, where it was also mentioned that "it was winter."

And it was at Jerusalem the feast of the dedication, and it was winter.

And Jesus walked in the temple in Solomon's porch.

(JOHN 10:22–23, KJV)

or

Then came the Festival of Dedication[] at Jerusalem. It was winter,

²³ and Jesus was in the temple courts walking in Solomon's Colonnade.

(JOHN 10:22, NIV)

Sky Signs in 2015

As it was described in the previous chapter the four Israelite summer feasts are not yet fulfilled; they are Feast of Trumpets, Day of Atonement, Feast of Tabernacles, and Feast of Hanukkah (Feast of Dedication). Surprisingly there were the signs in the sky which occurred on some of those feasts in 2015.

The Sky Signs and the End Times

On May 11, 1949, the independence of the State of Israel gained recognition from the United Nations.

The Lord Jesus said in Matthew 24:

³² Now learn a parable of the fig tree; **When his branch is yet tender, and putteth forth leaves, ye know that summer is nigh:**

THE RAPTURE

³³ So likewise ye, when ye shall see all these things, know that it is near, even at the doors.
*³⁴ Verily I say unto you, **This generation shall not pass, till all these things be fulfilled.***

Verse 32 explains: "When his branch is yet tender, and putteth forth leaves, ye know that summer is nigh:" which could be interpreted, "When the State of Israel is established," you know that "the fulfillment of the summer festivals is nigh," and then continued with the statement "Verily I say unto you, This generation shall not pass, till all these things be fulfilled" (verse 34). This could mean that the first generation or the people who lived in Israel at the time the State of Israel was established will not all pass away or die until the second coming of the Lord Jesus.

When the State of Israel got her independence, there were surely infants or children with their parents, and the verse explains that those infants and children will be still alive/remain when the Lord Jesus returns.

If we compute the time since the legal establishment of the State of Israel in 1949, the infants/children during that time will be about seventy years old at present. Now referring to Psalm 90:10:

*The days of our years are threescore years and ten; and if by reason of strength they be **fourscore years**, yet is their strength labour and sorrow; for it is soon cut off, and we fly away.*

Based on the interpretation of the above verses, the second coming of the Lord Jesus is imminent.

Fulfillment of the Year of Jubilee

The Israelites retrieved East Jerusalem on June 7, 1967, during the six-day war. Why is East Jerusalem so important? Because in East Jerusalem, there is a location believed to be the site of the Temple of God. Besides, East Jerusalem is God's promised land to the Israelites.

Many ministers believed that the rapture of the church should happen at the celebration of Jubilee. Actually, not many reasons were given, but it might simply be explained as follows:

"Is it possible that at later period during the rapture there will be children of God who still owe debts? In this sense those children of God are not unwilling to pay, but they are yet unable to pay or still have to pay off. About such children of God, can they be taken up or not? If they are taken up, they still have debts they need to pay. If not, they are God's children, aren't they?"

Most likely the answer is that they will be taken up, but first they have to pay off their debts. How do they pay them off? Can it be that God will give money to each of His children who still have debts? That is possible, but the debts may also be settled in the Year of Jubilee.

*But if he be not able to restore it to him, then that which is sold shall remain in the hand of him that hath bought it until the year of jubile: **and in the jubile it shall go out, and he shall return unto his possession**.*

(Lev 25:28)

THE RAPTURE

So if a man had to sell his land to someone else, he would get his land back in the Year of Jubilee, since his debt would be considered paid off or the price of the land settled in the Year of Jubilee.

Even if there was a poor man who sold himself to someone, he should be released or would regain his freedom in the Year of Jubilee.

And if thy brother that dwelleth by thee be waxen poor, and be sold unto thee; thou shalt not compel him to serve as a bond-servant: But as an hired servant, and as a sojourner, he shall be with thee, and shall serve thee unto the year of jubilee: And then shall he depart from thee, both he and his children with him, and shall return unto his own family, and unto the possession of his fathers shall he return.

(LEV 25:39–41)

If the rapture occurs in the Year of Jubilee, what method can we use to count this? How can the initial year toward the Year of Jubilee be determined?

The Book of Leviticus states that:

*And the LORD spake unto Moses in mount Sinai, saying, Speak unto the children of Israel, and say unto them, **When ye come into the land which I give you**, then shall the land keep a sabbath unto the LORD.*

(LEV 25:1–2)

So, the initial observance of the Sabbath as well as the Jubilee was when the Israelites entered the land given by the Lord, and this land was particularly East Jerusalem, the site of the Temple of God.

FULFILLMENT OF THE SUMMER FESTIVALS

If we count 49 years from June 7, 1967, the day the Israelites regained East Jerusalem, then add 49 x 360 days (1 biblical year) and it will point to **September 23, 2015, precisely on the Day of Atonement or Yom Kippur**.

2014		2015				
Apr - 15	Oct - 08	Mar - 20	Apr - 04	Sep - 13	Sep - 23	Sep - 28
		Sabbatical Year				
Nissan 14	Tishri 15	Nissan 1	Nissan 14	Tishri 1	Tishri 10	Tishri 15
Passover	Tabernacles	1st Cal.Year	Passover	Trumpets	Yom Kippur	Tabernacles

The Beginning of the End Times

At earlier stage it was explained that the Feast of Tabernacles will be fulfilled with phenomena related to the rapture of the Church. It is possible that the Feast of Tabernacles in the year 2015 which will occur on September 28 is related to the rapture since at that time it will have entered the celebration of Jubilee which starts in the evening of September 23.

If the phenomena connected with the rapture would occur during the Feast of Tabernacles in 2015, then the beginning of the end times should start three and a half years before September 28, 2015 or 1260 days before September 28, 2015, which would be on **April 16, 2012,**

in exact accordance with the celebration of the eighty-fifth birthday of Pope Benedictus XVI.

Many commentators believe that Daniel 9:27 is an early sign of the end times:

> *And he shall **confirm the covenant with many** for one week: and in the midst of the week he shall cause the sacrifice and the oblation to cease, and for the overspreading of abominations he shall make it desolate, even until the consummation, and that determined shall be poured upon the desolate.*
>
> (Da 9:27)

Some scholars interpreted that the covenant or agreement in this verse was an Israeli-Palestinian peace treaty.

The authors themselves are not of the same opinion since the verse clearly states that the covenant made by the king (antichrist) will become a heavy burden to "a lot of people," not only to the nation of Israel.

Furthermore the verse states that at that time he (the antichrist) **shall confirm the covenant**, emphasizing the tie of the agreement. It means at earlier time the agreement was already made, and at the appointed moment of the end times, **the antichrist just confirms that agreement**.

Previously, there was a speculation that Pope Benedictus XVI would resign at the age of eighty-five or on April 16, 2012. This turned up because Pope Benedictus XVI had earlier stated several times that a pope was not obliged to keep his official position until the end of his life, rather, be in it as long as he as Pope is able to perform his duties properly. Could it be that at the corresponding festive day,

FULFILLMENT OF THE SUMMER FESTIVALS

the antichrist made a contact and reconfirmed the plan of Pope Benedictus XVI to resign?

Why would the resignation of Pope Benedictus XVI become a burden to many people? Because his successor, as it has been prophesied, would be a false prophet or Petrus Romanus who would feed his people with a lot of miseries and bring destruction to Rome. (See *The Rapture, Fulfillment of: The Signs in the Sky, the Festivals in Summer, and the Parables of the End Times Part 1*, chapter IV.)

2012	2014		2015				
Apr - 16	Apr - 15	Oct - 08	Mar - 20	Apr - 04	Sep - 13	Sep - 23	Sep - 28
			Sabbatical Year				
	Nissan 14	Tishri 15	Nissan 1	Nissan 14	Tishri 1	Tishri 10	Tishri 15
	Passover	Tabernacles	1st Cal. Year	Passover	Trumpets	Yom Kippur	Tabernacles
early end of time						JUBILEE	

Purification and Rapture

Furthermore, if we link the above commentary about the beginning of the end times which started on April 16, 2012, with the Book of Daniel, then we will find a very surprising fact.

Daniel 12:12 states:

*Blessed is he that waiteth, and cometh to the **thousand three hundred and five and thirty days**.*

If the beginning of the end times started on April 16, 2012, and we add 1,335 days since that date, then it will fall on December 12, 2015, which **coincides with the enlightening of the seventh lamp (candle) during the Feast of Hanukkah/Chanukah.**

December 2015

Sunday	Monday	Tuesday	Wednesday	Thursday	Friday	Saturday
		1	2	3	4	5
6	7	8	9	10	11	12
13	14	15	16	17	18	19
20	21	22	23	24	25	26
27	28	29	30	31		

Previously, it has been described that Hanukkah is a celebration of purification of the Temple to sanctify it again.

1 Co 3:16 said, "Know ye not that ye are the temple of God, and that the Spirit of God dwelleth in you?"

When Daniel 12:12 is linked with the verse before, then:

Many shall be purified, and made white, and tried; but the wicked shall do wickedly: and none of the wicked shall understand; but the wise shall understand.

Blessed is he that waiteth, and cometh to the thousand three hundred and five and thirty days.

(Da 12:10,12)

FULFILLMENT OF THE SUMMER FESTIVALS

These verses seem to explain that there will be a time of purification for the children of God before they are taken up. And if there is a process of purification, then the children of God will be purified until the enlightening of the seventh lamp (candle) which means until perfect, since seven is the number often used as a symbol of perfection.

2012	2014		2015					
Apr - 16	Apr - 15	Oct - 08	Mar - 20	Apr - 04	Sep - 13	Sep - 23	Sep - 28	Dec - 12
				Sabbatical Year				
	Nissan 14	Tishri 15	Nissan 1	Nissan 14	Tishri 1	Tishri 10	Tishri 15	Kislev 30
	Passover	Tabernacles	1st Cal.Year	Passover	Trumpets	Yom Kippur	Tabernacles	Chanukah
						JUBILEE		
early end of time								Rapture

Fulfillment of the Feast of Tabernacles

If the rapture will occur at the Feast of Hanukkah in 2015, which will be on December 12, 2015, then what events connected with the rapture may happen during the Feast of Tabernacles in 2015?

If we notice the description of the Lord Jesus about the end times, particularly in Matthew 24:29–30:

> [29] *Immediately after the tribulation of those days shall the sun be darkened, and the moon shall not give her light, and the stars shall fall from heaven, and the powers of the heavens shall be shaken:*
> [30] *And then shall appear the sign of the Son of man in heaven: and then shall all the tribes of the earth mourn, and*

THE RAPTURE

they shall see the Son of man coming in the clouds of heaven *with power and great glory.*

If we observe more carefully the above verses, we will see that soon after the tribulation in those days, they shall see the Lord Jesus coming in the clouds.

The appearance of the Lord Jesus is also described in 1 Thess 4:

[15] For this we say unto you by the word of the Lord, that we which are alive and remain unto the coming of the Lord shall not prevent them which are asleep.

[16] For the Lord himself shall descend from heaven with a shout, with the voice of the archangel, and with the trump of God: and the dead in Christ shall rise first:

[17] Then we which are alive and remain shall be caught up together with them in the clouds, to meet the Lord in the air: and so shall we ever be with the Lord.

1 Th 4:15–17 explains that when the sign was given, then:

1. The archangel shall shout with a large voice.
2. The trumpet of God shall be heard.
3. The Lord himself shall descend from heaven.
4. The dead in Christ shall rise.

"**Then** we which are alive and remain shall be caught up together with them in the clouds, to meet the Lord in the air: and so shall we ever be with the Lord."

FULFILLMENT OF THE SUMMER FESTIVALS

This means that there will be **elapse** between the **time** when Jesus Christ is coming in the clouds and the time the children of God meet the Lord Jesus in the clouds.

When we examine the verses above, it might be that the time Jesus Christ coming in the clouds and the time we are taken up to meet the Lord will not happen at the same moment or the same time, but rather in sequence starting from:

- The appearance of the sign of the Son of man in the sky.
- The Son of man descends from heaven in the clouds.
- The dead in Christ shall rise.
- The believers who are still alive will be taken up together in the clouds to meet the Lord in the air.

Furthermore, then this is in accordance with the parable of Jesus concerning the ten virgins (Mt 25:1–13).

*Then shall **the kingdom of heaven** be likened unto ten virgins, which took their lamps, and went forth to **meet the bridegroom**.*

And five of them were wise, and five were foolish.

They that were foolish took their lamps and took no oil with them.

But the wise took oil in their vessels with their lamps.

While the bridegroom tarried, they all slumbered and slept.

*And at midnight **there was a cry made, Behold, the bridegroom cometh; go ye out to meet him**.*

THE RAPTURE

Then all those virgins rose, and trimmed their lamps.

And the foolish said unto the wise, Give us of your oil; for our lamps are gone out.

But the wise answered, saying, Not so; lest there be not enough for us and you: but go ye rather to them that sell, and buy for yourselves.

*And **while they went to buy, the bridegroom came**; and they that were ready went in with him to the marriage: and the door was shut.*

Afterward, came also the other virgins, saying, Lord, Lord, open to us.

But he answered and said, Verily I say unto you, I know you not.

Watch therefore, for ye know neither the day nor the hour wherein the Son of man cometh.

(MT 25:1–13)

From this parable, we can learn that:

- This parable depicts the Kingdom of Heaven.
- Those girls are to meet the bridegroom which can be interpreted as the Church preparing to meet the Lord Jesus.
- There is a sign in the form of voices cried out: Here is the bridegroom! Come out to meet him!
- Some time later (when all the girls get up, the foolish ones ask for some oil from the wise ones. But their requests are rejected and they have to leave to buy some oil). Then the bridegroom comes.
- They that were ready went in with him to the marriage.

FULFILLMENT OF THE SUMMER FESTIVALS

If the parable of the ten virgins is linked with Daniel 12:10:

*Many **shall be purified, and made white, and tried**; but the wicked shall do wickedly: and none of the wicked shall understand; but the wise shall understand.*

Then those verses further substantiate that most likely the coming of the Lord Jesus will be preceded by some sign and after that there will be a time when God's children are to be cleansed, purified to such an extent that they will be worthy to meet the Lord in the air.

But Dan 12:10 also explains that during the time of the cleansing and purification, many will be tried, which can be interpreted that in that period, many will face various tests, one of which might be persecution. The Feast of Trumpet will be the end of a heavy persecution (*Great Tribulation*), yet not the end of the entire persecution, and most likely after the Great Tribulation in Jerusalem, the persecution upon the believers will become even more intense around the world.

Daniel 12:10 further explains that the wicked will act wickedly and none of the wicked will understand. This could mean that the believers who continue to lead a secular life will not understand the phenomena of this test, the cleansing and the purification, since they have very little knowledge of the Word (oil). So eventually they will get lost, turn away from their faith, and be left behind.

2012	2014		2015					
Apr - 16	Apr - 15	Oct - 08	Mar - 20	Apr - 04	Sep - 13	Sep - 23	Sep - 28	Dec - 12
			Sabbatical Year					
	Nissan 14	Tishri 15	Nissan 1	Nissan 14	Tishri 1	Tishri 10	Tishri 15	Kislev 30
	Passover	Tabernacles	1st Cal.Year	Passover	Trumpets	Yom Kippur	Tabernacles	Chanukah
						JUBILEE		
early end of time								Rapture

Fulfillment of the Feast of Trumpets

As it has been explained earlier, the Feast of Trumpets was celebrated by the people of Israel with trumpet blasts to warn themselves so as not to worship the golden calf or idols. And there is a great possibility that most people particularly in Jerusalem will fall again into this same sin as they will be forced to worship the image of antichrist set up there or be killed if they refuse.

> *And deceiveth them that dwell on the earth by the means of those miracles which he had power to do in the sight of the beast; saying to them that dwell on the earth, **that they should make an image to the beast**, which had the wound by a sword, and did live. And he had power to give life unto the image of the beast, that the image of the beast should both speak, and cause that **as many as would not worship the image of the beast should be killed**.*

> (REV 13:14)

The Lord Jesus explained when the Great Tribulation in Jerusalem would come to an end:

FULFILLMENT OF THE SUMMER FESTIVALS

*Immediately after the tribulation of those days shall **the sun be darkened**, and **the moon shall not give her light**, and the stars **shall fall from heaven**, and **the powers of the heaven shall be shaken**.*

(MT 24:29)

The verse explains that right after the cessation of the great distress or the Great Tribulation, there will be signs in the sky as follows:

1. The sun shall be darkened.
2. The moon shall not give her light.
3. The stars shall fall from heaven (the sky).
4. The powers of the heavens shall be shaken.

Some very interesting issues can be disclosed regarding "the sun shall be darkened" and "the moon shall not give her light."

The Sun Will Be Darkened

In the earlier part of this book, it has been discussed that the solar eclipse would occur twice in the year 2015, on March 20 (the first day of Nisan) and the second one on September 13, at the Feast of Trumpets.

The two solar eclipses are different from each other. The first one on March 20 will be a **total solar eclipse**, so when it happens, the sun will be **completely dark** in the region where it occurs. The second one on September 13 will be **a partial solar eclipse**, so when it occurs, the sun will be seen **dim** in the region where it occurs. Very interestingly, in the King James Version, the verse about these events says "the sun will be darkened" or **be dimmed**, which means that it will not be totally dark.

THE RAPTURE

*Immediately after the tribulation of those days shall **the sun be darkened**, and the moon shall not give her light, and the stars shall fall from heaven, and the powers of the heavens shall be shaken.*

(MT 24:29)

Referring to these explanations, it is most possible that the partial solar eclipse on September 13, 2015, which will occur exactly at the Feast of Trumpets, is the intended sign in the sky.

The Moon Will Not Give Its Light

The same verse also explains that at the time when the sun will be dimmed, **the moon too will not give its light**. We know that the moon revolves around the earth every thirty days. During that time the moon will give its light as the reflection of the sun. Its light will increase day by day till it reaches its most intense illumination at **full moon**. Then the light of the moon will gradually decrease day by day till **it becomes totally dark fifteen days later, after the full moon**.

If we pay attention to both the solar eclipses above and the lunar eclipses that follow, the first solar eclipse will occur on the first day of Nisan, while the lunar eclipse on the fourteenth day of Nisan. So the appearance of the two eclipses will differ by fourteen days. At the time of the solar eclipse on the first day of Nisan, the moon will not be totally dark, which means that it only glimmers or is dim. But the second solar eclipse will occur on the first day of Tishri, while the lunar eclipse on the fifteenth day of Tishri. Thereby the difference will be exactly fifteen days. So when the solar eclipse occurs on the first day of Tishri or at the Feast of Trumpets, **the moon will not give its**

FULFILLMENT OF THE SUMMER FESTIVALS

light. This issue enhances the possibility that the partial solar eclipse at the Feast of Trumpets on September 13, 2015, would be the end of the Great Tribulation.

2012	2014		2015					
Apr - 16	Apr - 15	Oct - 08	Mar - 20	Apr - 04	Sep - 13	Sep - 23	Sep - 28	Dec - 12
	Sabbatical Year							
	Nissan 14	Tishri 15	Nissan 1	Nissan 14	Tishri 1	Tishri 10	Tishri 15	Kislev 30
	Passover	Tabernacles	1st Cal.Year	Passover	Trumpets	Yom Kippur	Tabernacles	Chanukah
						JUBILEE		
early end of time					End of Great Tribulation			Rapture

More interesting things happen when related to the verses below:

*And he shall confirm **the covenant with many for one week:** and **in the midst of the week he shall cause the sacrifice and the oblation to cease**, and for the overspreading of abominations he shall make it desolate, even until the consummation, and that determined shall be poured upon the desolate.*

(DA 9:27)

*And from the time that the daily sacrifice shall be taken away, and the abomination that maketh desolate set up, there shall be **a thousand two hundred and ninety days**.*

(DA 12:11)

From the two verses and the previous interpretation, we understand that:

67

THE RAPTURE

- The end times will last seven years or two periods of 1,260 days.
- The beginning of the end times started on April 16, 2012, in coincidence with the celebration of the eighty-fifth anniversary of Pope Benedict XVI.
- In the middle of the appointed seven years, the antichrist will stop the sacrifice and offering.
- From the time the daily sacrifice is abolished, the gods of abomination are set up. The cessation of the daily sacrifice will continue for 1,290 days.
- The middle of the appointed seven years will be exactly on September 28, 2015, at the celebration of the Feast of Tabernacles.

Since the cessation of the daily sacrifice will start from the middle of the seven years until the termination of the end times, which will be 1,290 days, while the second period of three and a half year will be 1,260 days, so the cessation of the daily sacrifice will start from 1,290–1,260 days, or 30 days before September 28, 2015, which will be on August 29, 2015.

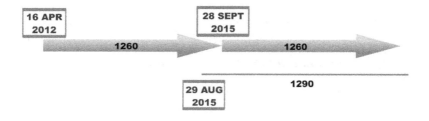

It has been explained previously that the Feast of Trumpets (first day of Tishri) is the first day of ten-day repentance called *Yamim*

Noraim, which ends on the Day of Atonement (*Yom Kippur/tenth day of Tishri*). The Feast of Trumpets is part of the *Teshuvah* which lasts for forty days (the turning back days). During the *Teshuvah* there are thirty days of preparation beginning from the first day of the sixth month (Elul), for a full month and ten days of *Yamim Noraim* to commemorate the event when Moses climbed Mount Sinai a second time to receive the Ten Commandments. For forty days they blew the trumpets to warn the people to be faithful to God and no longer worship idols (the golden calf made by Aaron).

The Feast of Trumpets conceives a prophecy that at the end times, the people of Israel would be challenged again to choose to worship idols, during the time of persecution or great distress (*Great Tribulation*). Antichrist will set up the idol of abomination (the beast) in Jerusalem and force the people of Judea to worship the image of "the sacred one" (the beast), and those who refuse to worship the image will be persecuted, even be killed.

> *And deceiveth them that dwell on the earth by the means of those miracles which he had power to do in the sight of the beast; saying to them that dwell on the earth, that they should make an image to the beast, which had the wound by a sword, and did live.*
>
> *And he had power to give life unto the image of the beast, that the image of the beast should both speak, and cause that as many as would not worship the image of the beast should be killed.*
>
> (REVELATION 13:14–15)

THE RAPTURE

So the forty days of Teshuvah starts on the first day of Elul or thirty days prior to the Feast of Trumpets; and Teshuvah for the year 2015 will begin on August 16, 2015. This means that when the daily sacrifice is abolished and the image of antichrist is to be set up on **August 29, 2015, the people of Israel will be in the Teshuvah**, the period when they have to turn back so as not to worship idols.

> *Fear none of those things which thou shalt suffer: behold, the devil shall cast some of you into prison, that ye may be tried; and ye shall have tribulation **ten days**: be thou faithful unto death, and I will give thee a crown of life.*
>
> (REV 2:10)

The verse above explains that the tribulation lasts for ten days, and if we count from the moment the image of antichrist is set up on August 29 until the end of the persecution period at the Feast of Trumpets on September 13, 2015, there will be sixteen days. Hence could it be possible that the ten days of great distress (Da 12:1) or the Great Tribulation (Mt 24:21) will occur during that time and will end on September 13, 2015?

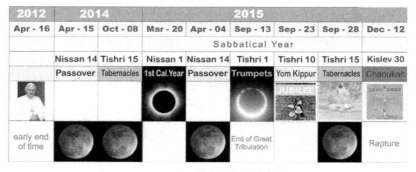

Great Tribulation (29/8-13/9)

FULFILLMENT OF THE SUMMER FESTIVALS

The End Times According to the Lord Jesus

The Lord Jesus described the events of the end times, among which we find in Matthew chapter 24, Mark chapter 13, and Luke chapter 17 and 21.

It is very interesting if we examine the sequence of events above and the one written in Mark 13. It seems that **both are similar**.

Mark 13:1
[1] And as he went out of the temple, one of his disciples saith unto him, Master, see what manner of stones and what buildings are here!

[2] And Jesus answering said unto him, Seest thou these great buildings? there shall not be left one stone upon another, that shall not be thrown down.

[3] And as he sat upon the mount of Olives over against the temple, Peter and James and John and Andrew asked him privately,

[4] Tell us, when shall these things be? and what shall be the sign when all these things shall be fulfilled?

[5] And Jesus answering them began to say, Take heed lest any man deceive you:

[6] For many shall come in my name, saying, I am Christ; and shall deceive many.

(There are many who are mislead today.)

[7] And when ye shall hear of wars and rumours of wars, be ye not troubled: for such things must needs be; but the end shall not be yet.

71

THE RAPTURE

⁸ᵃ For nation shall rise against nation, and kingdom against kingdom.

(The second seal/the red horse: conflict between God's people and people of other religions when the Temple of God will be rebuilt in Jerusalem)

And there went out another horse that was red: and power was given to him that sat thereon to take peace from the earth, and that they should kill one another: and there was given unto him a great sword.

(REV 6:4)

⁸ᵇ and there shall be earthquakes in divers places, and there shall be famines and troubles: these are the beginnings of sorrows.

(The third seal/ the black horse: the high price of various staple food)

⁹ But take heed to yourselves: for they shall deliver you up to councils; and in the synagogues ye shall be beaten: and ye shall be brought before rulers and kings for my sake, for a testimony against them.

(The people of God were persecuted by people of other religions.)

¹⁰ And the gospel must first be published among all nations.

FULFILLMENT OF THE SUMMER FESTIVALS

(Rev 14:6) And I saw another angel fly in the midst of heaven, having the everlasting gospel to preach unto them that dwell on the earth, and to every nation, and kindred, and tongue, and people.)

[11] But when they shall lead you, and deliver you up, take no thought beforehand what ye shall speak, neither do ye premeditate: but whatsoever shall be given you in that hour, that speak ye: for it is not ye that speak, but the Holy Ghost.

[12] Now the brother shall betray the brother to death, and the father the son; and children shall rise up against their parents, and shall cause them to be put to death. [13] And ye shall be hated of all men for my name's sake: but he that shall endure unto the end, the same shall be saved.

[14] But when ye shall see the abomination of desolation, spoken of by Daniel the prophet, standing where it ought not, - let him that readeth understand –

(Antichrist will be standing in the Temple of God in Jerusalem.)

then let them that be in Judaea flee to the mountains.

[15] And let him that is on the housetop not go down into the house, neither enter therein, to take any thing out of his house:

[16] And let him that is in the field not turn back again for to take up his garment.

[17] But woe to them that are with child, and to them that give suck in those days!

[18] And pray ye that your flight be not in the winter.

[19] For in those days shall be affliction, such as was not from the beginning of the creation which God created unto this time, either shall be.20 And except that the Lord had

THE RAPTURE

shortened those days, no flesh should be saved: but for the elect's sake, whom he hath chosen, he hath shortened the days.

(There will be a Great Tribulation/a period of great distress which coincides with the Teshuvah.)

[21] And then if any man shall say to you, Lo, here is Christ; or, lo, he is there; believe him not: For false Christ and false prophets shall rise, and shall shew signs and wonders, to seduce, if it were possible, even the elect.23 But take ye heed: behold, I have foretold you all things.

(False prophets will appear and perform great signs and false miracles.)

2 Th 2:9 The coming of the lawless one in accordance with the work of Satan displayed in all kinds of counterfeit miracles, signs and wonders.

[24] But in those days, after that tribulation, the sun shall be darkened, and the moon shall not give her light.

(Great Tribulation will end at the Feast of Trumpets.)

[25] And the stars of heaven shall fall, and the powers that are in heaven shall be shaken.

(Disasters related to the opening of the sixth seal)

[26] And then shall they see the Son of man coming in the clouds with great power and glory.

(The Lord Jesus will appear in the clouds at the Feast of Tabernacles.)

27 And then shall he send his angels, and shall gather together his elect from the four winds, from the uttermost part of the earth to the uttermost part of heaven.

(God's people will be caught up first by rising up those who died in Christ and followed by God's children who are still alive at the Feast of Hanukkah.)

Sky Signs in 2018–2019

Furthermore, in the year 2018–2019, there would occur three total lunar eclipses and four partial solar eclipses. As we study them further, it turns out that the three blood moons would happen at the Israelite festivals, which are at the **Feast of Tu Bishvat** and the **Feast of Tu B'av**.

			2018			2019	
Jan - 31	Feb - 15	Jul - 13	Jul - 27	Agt - 11	Jan - 06	Jan - 21	
Shevat 15			Av 15				Shevat 15
Tu Bishvat			Tu B'av				Tu Bishvat

The Feast of Tu Bishvat

The Feast of Tu Bishvat is **one of the four New Years** regarding the Israelite calendar, which begins on the fifteenth day of Shevat. The school of Hillel believes that the Israelite calendar starts on the fifteenth day of Shevat. The Israelites have four calendars—the first calendar begins on the first day of Nisan, the second begins on the fifteenth day of Shevat, the third begins on the first day of Tishri, and the fourth begins on the first day of Elul.

The Feast of Tu B'av

The Feast of Tu B'av is the **Feast of love**, which is an appropriate time for a wedding. So many Israelites get married at the Feast of Tu B'av. This feast day is a feast of joy celebrated in the Temple as a sign that the grape harvest has begun, which will end at the Feast of Yom Kippur. In both the feast days, the girls of Jerusalem would be dressed in white, which they borrow, and then they would dance in the vineyards.

Of all the Israelite festivals, there is none more exciting to the nation of Israel than the Feast of Tu B'av and Yom Kippur.

In the authors' opinion, the Feast of Tu B'av is connected with the **fifth seal** in Revelation 6:9–11:

> *⁹ And when he had opened the fifth seal, I saw under **the altar the souls of them that were slain** for the word of God, and for the testimony which they held:*
>
> *¹⁰ And they cried with a loud voice, saying, How long, O Lord, holy and true, dost thou not judge and avenge our blood on them that dwell on the earth?*

[11] *And **white robes** were given unto every one of them; and it was said unto them, that they should rest yet for a little season, until their fellowservants also and their brethren, that should be killed as they were, should be fulfilled.*

Why do we make such interpretation? Because they are given **white robes** just as the white dresses borrowed by the Israeli girls who dance at the Feast of Tu B'av.

And after the opening of the fifth seal, there was the rapture, when 144,000 Israelites were taken up from the earth as firstfruits offering to God and the Lamb. So before we would be taken up, the Israelites would be first, as many as 144,000 who were redeemed as the firstfruits offering.

The Israelites have four calendars. Let us examine two of them: One begins on the first day of Nisan and another begins on the fifteenth day of Shevat, or the Feast of Tu Bishvat. The calendar beginning on the first day of Nisan is based on the origin of the creation of the earth (www.torahcalendar.com), while the other beginning on the fifteenth of Shevat is based on the departure (exodus) of the Israelites from the land of Egypt, as written in Exodus 12:1–2:

[1] *And the LORD spake unto Moses and Aaron in the land of Egypt, saying,*

[2] *This month shall be unto you the beginning of months: it shall be **the first month of the year** to you.*

Now let us compare the chart or graphic of the signs in the sky of the year 2015–2016 with the one of the year 2018–2019. Both equally start from the beginning of the Jewish calendar, the first day of Nisan and the fifteenth day of Shevat. There we will see a very amazing issue—both charts have the same interval of days: 15–15, 177–177, and 192–192. Everything is exactly similar.

Now let us examine them one by one:

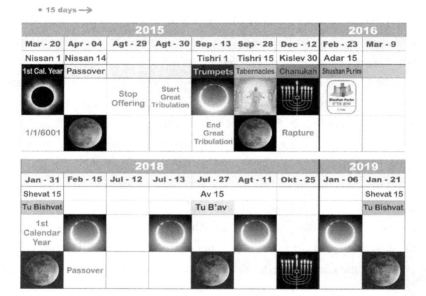

The interval of time from March 20 to April 4, 2015, and from January 31 to February 15, 2018, was equally fifteen days, or fourteen **days if reckoned from the Jewish calendar**, because in the Israelite calendar, one day starts from the evening until the next evening in accordance with what is written in Genesis 1:5:

> *And God called the light Day, and the darkness he called Night.* ***And the evening and the morning*** *were the first day.*

Since the Jewish calendar year beginning on the first day of Nisan is on March 20 while the fifteenth day of Shevat is January 31, and

FULFILLMENT OF THE SUMMER FESTIVALS

both start in the **evening** and then reckoned till April 4 and February 15 evening, **the interval would be fourteen days**. And the LORD God commanded the Israelites to celebrate the Passover on the fourteenth day from the beginning of the year, as stated in Lev 23:5:

In the fourteenth day of the first month *at even is the LORD's passover.*

Therefore, if the fourteenth day of Nisan is the Feast of Passover based on the calendar which begins on the first day of Nisan, then **February 15 is the Feast of Passover based on the calendar which begins on the fifteenth day of Shevat.**

Furthermore, the interval of days from March 20, 2015, to September 13, 2015, and from January 31, 2018, to July 27, 2018, is equal too, namely, 177 days.

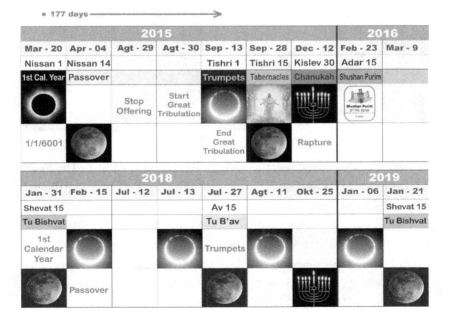

THE RAPTURE

In accordance with the above principle, **July 27, 2018, would then be the Feast of Trumpets, based on the calendar which starts on the fifteenth day of Shevat**.

Similarly, the interval of days from March 20, 2015, to September 28, 2015, and from January 31, 2018, to August 11, 2018, is equal too, namely, 192 days.

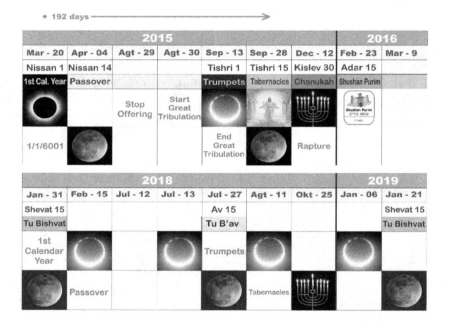

By the same principle, then **August 11, 2018, would be the Feast of Tabernacles based on the calendar which starts on the fifteenth day of Shevat**.

Therefore, if based on our calculations that August 29, 2015, or 162 days since the first day of Nisan was the day the daily sacrifice began to be abolished, and the image of antichrist was set up in Jerusalem as recorded in the Book of Daniel and the Book of Revelation, could it be true that 162 days after the fifteenth day of Shevat, this event would take place?

FULFILLMENT OF THE SUMMER FESTIVALS

*And from the time that the daily sacrifice shall be taken away, and **the abomination that maketh desolate set up**, there shall be a thousand two hundred and ninety days.*

(DANIEL 12:11)

*And deceiveth them that dwell on the earth by the means of those miracles which he had power to do in the sight of the beast; saying to them that dwell on the earth, that they **should make an image to the beast, which had the wound by a sword**, and did live.*

(REVELATION 13:14)

• 162 days ⟶

2015							2016	
Mar - 20	Apr - 04	Agt - 29	Agt - 30	Sep - 13	Sep - 28	Dec - 12	Feb - 23	Mar - 9
Nissan 1	Nissan 14			Tishri 1	Tishri 15	Kislev 30	Adar 15	
1st Cal. Year	Passover			Trumpets	Tabernacles	Chanukah	Shushan Purim	
1/1/6001		Stop Offering	Start Great Tribulation	End Great Tribulation		Rapture		

2018							2019	
Jan - 31	Feb - 15	Jul - 12	Jul - 13	Jul - 27	Agt - 11	Okt - 25	Jan - 06	Jan - 21
Shevat 15				Av 15				Shevat 15
Tu Bishvat				Tu B'av				Tu Bishvat
1st Calendar Year								
	Passover	Stop Offering						

THE RAPTURE

On July 13, 2018, or the day after the daily sacrifice would be abolished and the image of antichrist would be set up, a partial solar eclipse would occur. What significant event could take place on that day? When we read Revelation 13:15, the image or statue of antichrist would not only be set up in Jerusalem, but there would be a demand that the entire population of the earth should worship the image of antichrist, and if they refuse, they would be killed.

*And he had power to give life unto the image of the beast, that the image of the beast should both speak, **and cause that as many as would not worship the image of the beast should be killed.***

(REVELATION 13:15, KJV)

or

*He was given power to give breath to the image of the first beast, so that it could speak and **cause all who refused to worship the image to be killed.***

(NIV)

In connection with the establishment of the statue of antichrist, the Lord Jesus gave a more detailed explanation that the antichrist would not only have the image of himself to be worshiped, but he would stand in the Temple of God and declare himself as god. And the people of Israel who are in Jerusalem would be forced to worship his image and acknowledge him as god; meanwhile he would persecute anyone who refuses to do so. Therefore most likely the solar eclipse seen on this date/day is connected with the Great Tribulation or severe persecutions which are to occur in Jerusalem.

FULFILLMENT OF THE SUMMER FESTIVALS

When ye therefore shall see the abomination of desolation, spoken of by Daniel the prophet, stand in the holy place, (whoso readeth, let him understand:)

Then let them which be in Judaea flee into the mountains

Let him which is on the housetop not come down to take any thing out of his house

Neither let him which is in the field return back to take his clothes.

And woe unto them that are with child, and to them that give suck in those days!

But pray ye that your flight be not in the winter, neither on the sabbath day.

For then shall be great tribulation, such as was not since the beginning of the world to this time, no, nor ever shall be.

And except those days should be shortened, there should no flesh be saved: but for the elect's sake those days shall be shortened.

(MT 24:15–22)

*And he shall confirm the covenant with many for one week: and in the midst of the week he shall cause the sacrifice and the oblation to cease, **and for the overspreading of abominations he shall make it desolate**, even until the consummation, and that determined shall be poured upon the desolate.*

(DANIEL 9:27)

*And arms shall stand on his part, and they **shall pollute the sanctuary** of strength, and shall take away the daily sacrifice, and they **shall place the abomination that maketh desolate**.*

(DANIEL 11:31, KJV)

83

THE RAPTURE

or

His armed forces will rise up to desecrate the temple fortress and will abolish the daily sacrifice. Then they will set up the abomination that causes desolation.

(NIV)

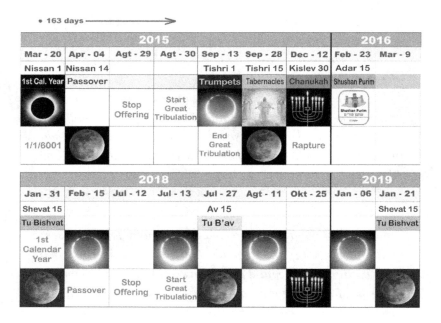

Furthermore, 267 days since the first day of Nisan or **266 days according to Jewish Calendar** would be the Feast of Hanukkah, and to our interpretation on that day, the believers will be caught up to meet the Lord in the air as described in 1 Thessalonians 4:17:

FULFILLMENT OF THE SUMMER FESTIVALS

*Then **we which are alive** and remain shall be **caught up together with them in the clouds, to meet the Lord in the air**: and so shall we ever be with the Lord.*

● 267 days ───────────────────────────────→

	2015						2016	
Mar - 20	Apr - 04	Agt - 29	Agt - 30	Sep - 13	Sep - 28	Dec - 12	Feb - 23	Mar - 9
Nissan 1	Nissan 14			Tishri 1	Tishri 15	Kislev 30	Adar 15	
1st Cal. Year	Passover			Trumpets	Tabernacles	Chanukah	Shushan Purim	
		Stop Offering	Start Great Tribulation					
1/1/6001				End Great Tribulation		Rapture		

	2018						2019	
Jan - 31	Feb - 15	Jul - 12	Jul - 13	Jul - 27	Agt - 11	Okt - 25	Jan - 06	Jan - 21
Shevat 15				Av 15				Shevat 15
Tu Bishvat				Tu B'av				Tu Bishvat
1st Calendar Year				Trumpets		Rapture		
	Passover	Stop Offering	Start Great Tribulation		Tabernacles			

The last solar eclipse would occur on January 6, 2019, 340 days after the fifteenth day of Shevat or Tu Bishvat. What significant event could take place in connection with this sign in the sky? Whereas the signs in the sky of 2018–2019 are the repetition of the ones of 2015–2016, so referring to the calculations and interpretations made in 2015–2016, they would be fulfilled in 2018–2019. When we reckon 340 days since the first day of Nisan in 2015, it would be on the **fifteenth day of Adar**/February 23, 2016, at **the Feast of Shushan Purim**. Therefore, based on the calendar which starts on the fifteenth day of Shevat, January 6, 2019, would also be at the Feast of Shushan Purim. The Feast of Purim is a feast day to commemorate

85

THE RAPTURE

the retaliation against those people in the past who had persecuted the Israelites. Could it be at this Feast of Shushan Purim that the seventh seal would be opened, concerning the days of vengeance allowed by God toward those who persecute His people, by beginning to pour out the vials of the God's wrath upon those left on earth? Revelation 16:1 states:

And I heard a great voice out of the temple saying to the seven angels, Go your ways, and pour out the vials of the wrath of God upon the earth.

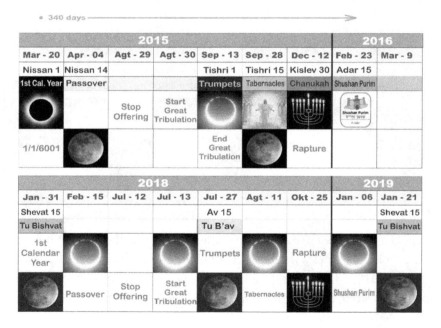

So overall the comparisons and similarities concerning the interval of days between the signs in the sky of the year 2015 and the year 2018 are as follows:

FULFILLMENT OF THE SUMMER FESTIVALS

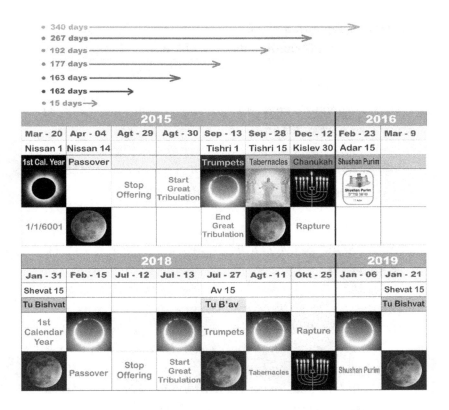

If we observe the signs in the sky of 2015 and of 2018, there are similarities in the interval of days in both periods, between each sign in the sky of 2015 and its matching pair of 2018. Regarding the signs in the sky we observed, the ones in 2015 are similar with those in 2018, and vice versa. So we can see similar signs in the sky and similar Israelite's festivals in both years, reinforced by the fact that each pair of those signs in the sky in both periods is different from each other. If in the year 2015 the solar eclipse took place, then its matching pair in the year 2018 would be a lunar eclipse, and vice versa.

Therefore, in our opinion, the signs in the sky of the year 2018 are

THE RAPTURE

the **review** or **repetition** of the ones in the year 2015. God gives those signs twice as **an affirmation** that **He will make it happen soon**.

Genesis 41:17
And Pharaoh said unto Joseph, In my dream, behold, I stood upon the bank of the river:

*[18] And, behold, there came up out of the river **seven kine, fatfleshed and well favoured**; and they fed in a meadow:*

*[19] And, behold, **seven other kine came up after them, poor and very ill favoured and leanfleshed**, such as I never saw in all the land of Egypt for badness:*

[20] And the lean and the ill favoured kine did eat up the first seven fat kine:

[21] And when they had eaten them up, it could not be known that they had eaten them; but they were still ill favoured, as at the beginning. So I awoke.

*[22] And I saw in my dream, and, behold, **seven** ears came up in one stalk, full and good:*

*[23] And, behold, **seven ears, withered, thin, and blasted with the east wind, sprung up after them**:*

[24] And the thin ears devoured the seven good ears: and I told this unto the magicians; but there was none that could declare it to me.

*[25] And Joseph said unto Pharaoh, **The dream of Pharaoh is one**: God hath shewed Pharaoh what he is about to do.*

*[26] **The seven good kine are seven years; and the seven good ears are seven years: the dream is one.***

[27] And the seven thin and ill favoured kine that came up after them are seven years; and the seven empty ears blasted with the east wind shall be seven years of famine.

FULFILLMENT OF THE SUMMER FESTIVALS

²⁸ This is the thing which I have spoken unto Pharaoh: What God is about to do he sheweth unto Pharaoh.

²⁹ Behold, there come seven years of great plenty throughout all the land of Egypt:

³⁰ And there shall arise after them seven years of famine; and all the plenty shall be forgotten in the land of Egypt; and the famine shall consume the land;

³¹ And the plenty shall not be known in the land by reason of that famine following; for it shall be very grievous.

*³² **And for that the dream was doubled unto Pharaoh twice; it is because the thing is established by God, and God will shortly bring it to pass.***

Or ***The reason the dream was given to Pharaoh in two forms is that the matter has been firmly decided by God, and God will do it soon***.

(NIV)

Verse 32 above explains that the repetition for the second time means *the thing is established by God, and God will shortly bring it to pass*

(KJV)

Or *the matter has been firmly decided by God, and God will do it soon*

(NIV)

Thus the Lord would first give **the signs in the sky** as recorded in Acts 2:20: "**The sun shall be turned into darkness**, and **the moon into blood**, before that great and notable day of the Lord come."

2014		2015				
Apr - 15	Oct - 08	Mar - 20	Apr - 04	Sep - 13	Sep - 23	Sep - 28
		Sabbatical Year				
Nissan 14	Tishri 15	Nissan 1	Nissan 14	Tishri 1	Tishri 10	Tishri 15
Passover	Tabernacles	1st Cal. Year	Passover	Trumpets	Yom Kippur	Tabernacles

Then the explanation was given beforehand so that we would understand the meaning of those signs in the sky and the prophecies related to the Israelite festivals. Hence we can prepare ourselves better for the Lord Jesus' second coming.

2015						
Mar - 20	Apr - 04	Agt - 29	Agt - 30	Sep - 13	Sep - 28	Dec - 12
Nissan 1	Nissan 14			Tishri 1	Tishri 15	Kislev 30
1st Cal. Year	Passover	Stop Offering	Start Great Tribulation	Trumpets	Tabernacles	Chanukah
1/1/6001				End Great Tribulation		Rapture

FULFILLMENT OF THE SUMMER FESTIVALS

And later the signs in the sky will be **repeated** to occur and be seen in the year 2018, as God's revelation that He has affirmed or substantiated the second coming of the Lord Jesus through the **fulfillment of the Israelite summer festivals**.

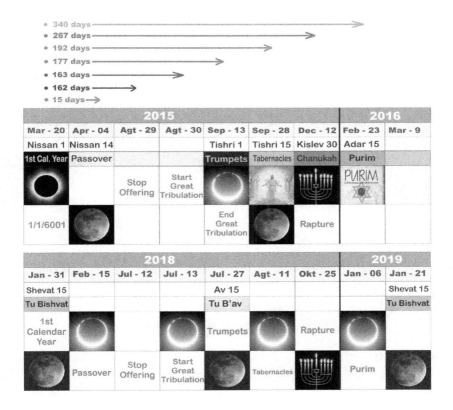

CHAPTER 4

FULFILLMENT OF THE
PARABLES OF THE END TIMES

Genesis 41:32 quoted previously also explains that the doubled signs, namely, repeated twice, bears the understanding or perception that **God will do it soon**.

And when would it take place, this "soon" mentioned in that verse?

The parable of the barren fig tree in Luke13:6–9 might be able to explain the time when God would do it.

He spake also this parable; A certain man had a fig tree planted in his vineyard; and he came and sought fruit thereon, and found none.

*Then said he unto the dresser of his vineyard, Behold, **these three years** I come seeking fruit on this fig tree, and find none: cut it down; why cumbereth it the ground?*

*And he answering said unto him, Lord, **let it alone this year also**, till I shall **dig** about it, and **dung it**:*

THE RAPTURE

And if it bear fruit, well: and if not, then after that thou shalt cut it down.

(LUKE 13:6–9)

The Lord Jesus referred briefly to **the above parable** when He explained about the end of the age,

*Now learn **a parable of the fig tree**; When his branch is yet tender, and putteth forth leaves, ye know that summer is nigh.*

(MATT 24:32)

This means that the fig tree in both parables is the same, namely, **referring to the Israelites**. So the parable in Luke 13 could be interpreted as such that for three years since the year 2015 till 2018, the Lord had given some signs of His second coming, either through signs in the sky or any other signs to remind the people of Israel to repent and receive Jesus Christ as Lord and Savior. But they did not repent. Then the Lord in His grace prolongs by another year their opportunity to repent which is the year 2019. And this condition applies to us too, the spiritual Israelites. We are given the chance to truly repent and prepare ourselves to greet His coming. It is said that during this ultimate additional year, *I (the gardener) will **dig** around it, and **fertilize** it* (NIV).

The gardener dug the ground and fertilized it to make the soil fertile so that the trees will bear fruit abundantly as mentioned in "the Parable of the Sower." This can be interpreted that in this one last year, the Lord would correct, discipline or rebuke, and smite or strike, even allow afflictions or distress (*to dig the ground*), but would also grant grace and give many very clear signs of the end times (*to fertilize*), for the people of Israel and us to repent.

94

FULFILLMENT OF THE PARABLES OF THE END TIMES

Sky Signs in 2019–2020

Before the second coming of the Lord, God still gave the last signs of blood moon at the beginning of year 2019 of fifteenth Shevat calendar and three other eclipses in days related to the end-time events.

When we observe closely the signs in the sky and the Israelite festivals according to the calendar which starts on the fifteenth day of Shevat, we will discover several amazing things:

1. On July 2, 2019, the day we interpret as when the daily sacrifice was abolished and the statue of the antichrist was set up in God's Holy Temple in Jerusalem, **the total solar eclipse (the sun darkened)** occurred.
2. After the statue of the antichrist was set up, the antichrist will force the people in Jerusalem to worship the statue, and those who refuse to do so will be killed, and this great tribulation will continue for ten days. After this severe torture, **a natural phenomenon will be seen showing the darkened moon**.

   *Immediately after the tribulation of those days shall the sun be darkened and **the moon shall not give her light**, and the stars shall fall from heaven, and the powers of the heavens shall be shaken.*

   (MT 24:29)

   On July 16, 2019, **a partial lunar eclipse** occurred as the moon became dark shaded by the earth. Is it possible that this eclipse was the one referred to in the verse?
3. The Feast of Purim is a feast day to commemorate the event the Jews experienced in the era Ester was queen of King

THE RAPTURE

Ahasuerus, ruler over Persia and Media. During that time Haman son of Hammedatha had made a plot to kill all the Jews in that kingdom on the thirteenth day of Adar. But what happened of his evil plan was the reverse. Haman himself was hanged on the gallow he prepared for Mordechai, the Jew he hated very much, when Ester the queen, Mordechai's cousin, displayed Haman's plot to the king. And at the appointed day that Haman had settled to carry out his evil plan, the situation turned to the contrary since the Jews were allowed to defend themselves and to take vengeance to kill those who hate them. In the citadel of Shushan, the killing of them who hated the Jews continued even to the next day, the fourteenth day of Adar. Since then the Jews commemorate this event every year on the fourteenth and the fifteenth day of Adar.

And Mordecai wrote these things, and set letters unto all the Jews that were in all the provinces of the king Ahasuerus, both nigh and far.

To establish this among them, that they should keep the fourteenth day of the month Adar, and the fifteenth day of the same, yearly,

As the days wherein the Jews rested from their enemies, and the month which was turned unto them from sorrow to joy, and from mourning into a good day: that they should make them days of feasting and joy, and of sending portions one to another, and gifts to the poor.

(ESTHER 9:20–22)

FULFILLMENT OF THE PARABLES OF THE END TIMES

On December 26, 2019, the fourteenth day of Adar, whence in the era of Ester the Jews were allowed to retaliate the cruelty of their haters, the **annular solar eclipse** will occur and the sun will be dimmed. Could it be that on that very day, **the trumpet would be blown/the first vial or bowl of God's wrath** would be poured out as the retaliation for the cruelty of those who had persecuted the Israelites?

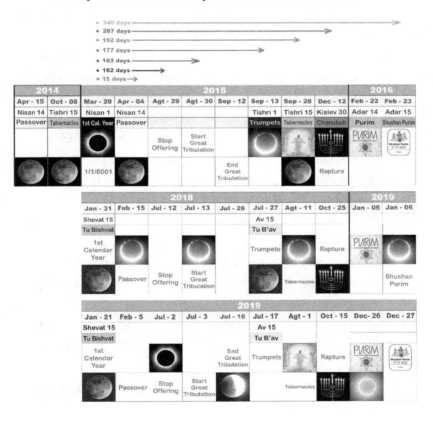

Furthermore, when we observe the graphic of eclipses and the Israelite feast days or festivals, also the days connected to the end times, we will see the amazing fact that **at almost all those days, we see the occurrence of the signs in the sky**!

1. At the time of the Passover, April 15, 2014, **the total lunar eclipse occurred**.
2. At the Feast of Tabernacles, October 8, 2014, **the total lunar eclipse occurred**.
3. At the beginning of the year/on the first day of the month Nisan, March 20, 2015, **the total solar eclipse occurred**.
4. At the beginning of the year/on the fifteenth day of the month Shevat, January 31, 2018, **the total lunar eclipse occurred**.
5. At the beginning of the year/on the fifteenth day of the month Shevat, January 21, 2019, **the total lunar eclipse occurred**.
6. At the time of the Passover, April 4, 2015, **the total lunar eclipse occurred**.
7. At the time of the Passover, February 15, 2018, **the partial solar eclipse occurred**.
8. On the day we interpreted/presumed as when the daily sacrifice was abolished, July 2, 2019, **the total solar eclipse occurred**.
9. On the day we interpreted/presumed as the beginning of the Great Tribulation in Jerusalem, July 13, 2018, **the partial solar eclipse occurred**.
10. On the day of the Feast of Trumpets, September 13, 2015, **the partial solar eclipse occurred**.
11. On the day of the Feast of Trumpets, July 27, 2018, **the total lunar eclipse occurred**.

FULFILLMENT OF THE PARABLES OF THE END TIMES

12. One day before the Feast of Trumpets, July 16, 2019, presumed to be the day of the cessation of the persecution in Jerusalem, **the partial lunar eclipse will occur**.
13. At the Feast of Tabernacles, September 28, 2015, **the total lunar eclipse occurred**.
14. At the Feast of Tabernacles, August 11, 2018, **the partial solar eclipse occurred**.
15. At the Feast of Shushan Purim, on January 6, 2019, **the partial solar eclipse will occur**.
16. At the Feast of Purim (fourteenth day of Adar), December 26, 2019, **the annular solar eclipse will occur**.

The verse in Acts 2:20 states, "The sun shall be turned into darkness, and the moon into blood, **before** that great and notable day of the Lord come."

The above verse explains that the end times will occur after the entire solar eclipse and blood moon are complete!

The last eclipse in the form of an annular solar eclipse will occur on December 26, 2019.

Therefore it is very possible that the second coming of the Lord Jesus and the accompanying events will be the fulfillment of the summer feasts of Israel based on the calendar of the fifteenth of Shevat 2020:

THE RAPTURE

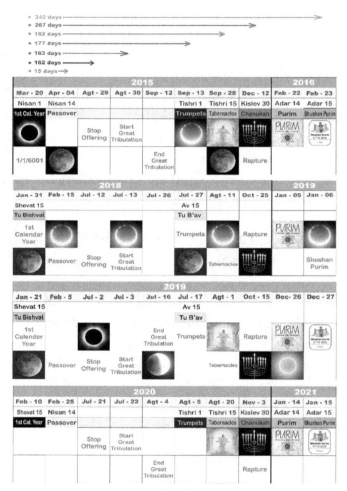

or based on the calendar the first of Nisan in 2020:

FULFILLMENT OF THE PARABLES OF THE END TIMES

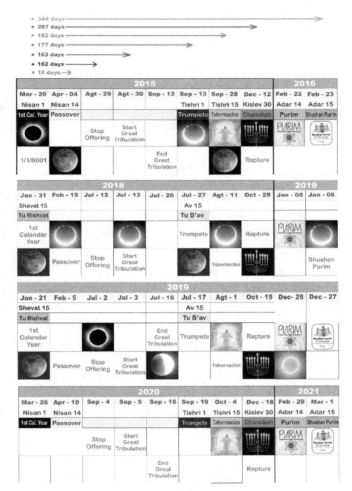

www.wahyuakhirzaman.com

The last days before the coming of the Lord Jesus will begin with the emergence of antichrist, namely, a world leader whose head is wounded by a sword is expected to die but still alive. Then the Temple of God will be built in Jerusalem but will get extraordinary opposition from Muslims. As a result, there will be a war between the state of Israel and Islamic countries which then extends into a worldwide dispute between Jews, Christians, and Catholics on the one hand with Muslims on the other. This fight was so powerful that they would kill each other.

Labor Pains

Nowadays, there are still God's children and even God's servants who don't believe that we are in the last days before the coming of the Lord Jesus because the world is currently in a state of peace and security. There is no visible phenomenon of chaos or fierce war that can be a sign that we are at the end of the end times.

The Bible records that the end times will occur when conditions are safe and peaceful, but they will suddenly turn into chaos accompanied by severe persecution.

1 Thessalonians 5:3 states"
For when they shall say, Peace and safety; then sudden destruction cometh upon them, as travail upon a woman with child; and they shall not escape.

(KJV)

or

While people are saying, 'Peace and safety,' destruction will come on them suddenly, as labor pains on a pregnant woman, and they will not escape.

(NIV)

So before the second coming of the Lord Jesus, the situation will be safe and peaceful. But suddenly the situation will change, which is analogized to a pregnant woman overwrought by birth pangs, namely something extraordinary that happens unexpectedly. We know that before the delivery, pregnant women will experience travail or pangs of childbirth, which is actually muscular contractions with tremendous pain. Those contractions occur suddenly, and we can not tell when they will start and for how long. However, it is indeed for only a short time, and after the child is born, the tremendous pain ceases.

The authors interpret the situation at the end times in connection with the above verse as follows: The end times would take place when the situation is peaceful and safe, thus, not when a great battle is going on, for example, the third world war. But then some event occurs that will change the peaceful and safe condition into a state of turmoil with severe persecutions against God's people. This period would not last long, though, and after that period of persecutions, the people of God who remain steadfast in their faith would be caught up in the air to meet the Lord Jesus, and at that exact moment, the era of God's grace bestowed to mankind would end.

We know that the **normal gestation period lasts 266 days** and the Lord gave a lot of signs similar to pregnancy.

Here below are those signs:

THE RAPTURE

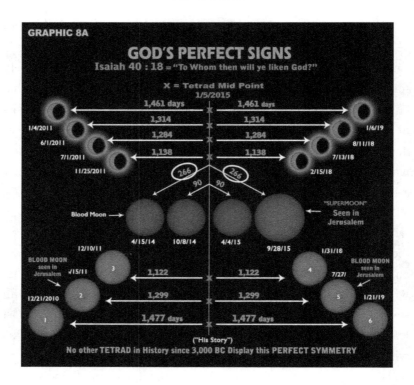

If we look at the perfect signs in the sky shown above, from the midpoint to the lunar eclipse on April 15, 2014, the interval is 266 days and also to the lunar eclipse on September 28, 2015, exactly 266 days!

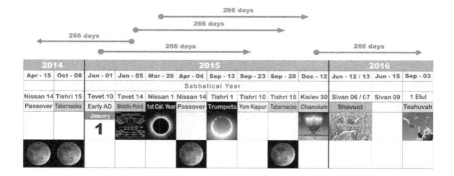

FULFILLMENT OF THE PARABLES OF THE END TIMES

In addition, there are three other occasions which have the interval of 266 days, namely:

1. January 1, to Yom Kippur on September 23, 2015.
2. March 20 (first day of Nisan), the beginning of Israelite calender to the Feast of Hanukkah on December 12, 2015.
3. Feast of Hanukkah to the first day of Elul, September 3, 2016. The first day of Elul is the first day of Teshuvah or the period to repent before entering the Feast of Trumpets and the celebration of Yom Kippur.

And besides, **the present Pope Franciscus is the 266th pope**! In the year 2015, he visited the White House on the 266th day, September 23, 2015, in coincidence with the celebration of Yom Kippur.

CHAPTER 5

CONCLUSION

The appearance of the signs in the sky and their connection with the Israelite festivals which were so precise that did not miss even a single day should make us aware that the coming of the Lord Jesus is so close and imminent. Therefore we have to prepare ourselves as soon and as seriously as possible to deal with that fact. There are at least three things we need to do at this time, which are as follows:

Reading the Bible Diligently

In his book *The Heaviest Temptations*, Yunus Ciptawilangga explained that the heaviest temptations or trials in human life are in fact not starvation, persecution, or imprisonment, but abstract ones that are not obvious, such as twisted Word of God or verses which succeeded to cause Adam and Eve fall into sin. The Lord Jesus too was tempted with the same temptation, but He won. Why? Because He understood! When Satan said, "If thou be the Son of God, command that these stones be made bread" (Mt 4:3), the Lord Jesus refused to

THE RAPTURE

do so, because He understood that, "Man shall not live by bread alone, but by every word that proceedeth out of the mouth of God" (Mat 4:4).

In the last days, many false prophets would spring up to mislead the people of God. If our faith is not deep rooted, which means having no profound knowledge of the Word of God and no experience of living close to Him, then we would be easily deceived by Satan like the five foolish virgins, who had no oil in their jars. At the end times, Satan would use his wiles to mislead God's children to apostasy.

> *And such as do wickedly against the covenant **shall he corrupt by flatteries**: but the people that **do know their God** shall be strong, and do exploits.*
>
> (DANIEL 11:32, KJV)

or

> ***With flattery he will corrupt those who have violated the covenant**, but the people **who know their God** will firmly resist him.*
>
> (DANIEL 11:32, NIV)

So we have to seriously make good use of this remaining time to study God's Word diligently.

Reserving Quiet Time

We should initiate and improve our quiet times with the Lord. Set aside enough time to pray to the LORD God for His wisdom and strength, so that we would be enabled to understand the Word of God and be granted the strength to apply God's Word in our lives.

CONCLUSION

But the end of all things is at hand: be ye therefore sober, and watch unto prayer.

(1 PE. 4:7)

Taking Care of Our Family

We must take good care of our families. Most importantly, let us make sure that none in our families has not accepted the Lord Jesus Christ as his/her personal Savior and Lord, for He alone can guarantee us to have eternal life with Him in heaven. He was the only One ordained by the LORD God to become our Redeemer through His sacrifice on the cross. He died then, was buried, and rose again on the third day and is now glorified in heaven, for that is why the Holy Spirit descends to fill the people who believe in Jesus Christ.

In addition, if we have problems today, we can share the burden with the servants of God or the church council or vestry. However, at the end of time, when we are entering the period of persecution and have to run as described in Matthew 10:23,

But when they persecute you in this city, flee ye into another: for verily I say unto you, Ye shall not have gone over the cities of Israel, till the Son of man be come,

apparently we would all run to our respective destinations. We may not be able to run with pastors and friends of our faith. If we are fortunate and can run with our families, then only our family members are left who can become a place to share our burdens.

THE RAPTURE

Overcoming the Fear

Fear is always part of the struggles in one's life, especially toward the end of the world when we will have to risk our lives. We must control and manage this fear in us so that it can be converted into a motivation to do useful things. First, definitely we must have a personal relationship with Jesus Christ to obtain the assurance of eternal life that we may receive God's forgiveness and will be granted to enter the eternal life with Him hereafter. If God is our Father, there is nothing to worry.

Fear not, little flock; for it is your Father's good pleasure to give you the kingdom.

(LK. 12:32)

Second, every Christian should have a prominent life worthy of the calling we have received in Christ. In Ephesians 4:1–3 the Apostle Paul admonishes us:

I therefore, the prisoner of the Lord, beseech you, that ye walk worthy of the vocation wherewith ye are called,
² With all lowliness and meekness, with longsuffering, forbearing one another in love.
³ Endeavouring to keep the unity of the Spirit in the bond of peace.

To know Christ and live according to His will would eradicate the fear.

Third, what will happen actually at the end of time is something encouraging.

CONCLUSION

First, 1 Thessalonians 4:13–18 records:

¹³ But I would not have you to be ignorant, brethren, concerning them which are asleep, that ye sorrow not, even as others which have no hope.

¹⁴ For if we believe that Jesus died and rose again, even so them also which sleep in Jesus will God bring with him.

¹⁵ For this we say unto you by the word of the Lord, that we which are alive and remain unto the coming of the Lord shall not prevent them which are asleep.

¹⁶ For the Lord himself shall descend from heaven with a shout, with the voice of the archangel, and with the trump of God: and the dead in Christ shall rise first:

¹⁷ Then we which are alive and remain shall be caught up together with them in the clouds, to meet the Lord in the air: and so shall we ever be with the Lord.

¹⁸ Wherefore comfort one another with these words.

Instead of facing the coming persecution with fear, we are called to anticipate the future with joy. Why? Because in Christ we will be "caught up" and so we "will be with the Lord forever." Isn't that something wonderful that should encourage us?

Furthermore, the Scripture says that we need not fear the Day of Judgment:

Herein is our love made perfect, that we may have boldness in the day of judgment: because as he is, so are we in this world.

There is no fear in love; but perfect love casteth our fear: because fear hath torment. He that feareth is not made perfect in love.

(1 Jn.4:17–18)

THE RAPTURE

The Apostle Peter said that even if we in the future have to face sufferings, we need not fear:

But and if ye suffer for righteousness' sake, happy are ye: and be not afraid of their terror, neither be troubled.

(1 PE. 3:14)

Peter and many believers suffered manifold persecutions in their lives and even face death for their faith in Christ. Suffering is not to be feared; suffering is a blessing if it becomes a testimony to the glory of the Lord Jesus' name.

People who do not know Christ do not have the promise of peace in the future. For them, it is a big problem because they have not obtained any assurance of salvation whenever they should enter the life hereafter. Those who know Christ are not afraid to face the last days of the world. On the contrary, we seek to live worthy of His calling, live in faith, endure our sufferings patiently, anticipating the second coming of Christ, and rest upon the conviction that our days are in His hands.

My times are in thy hand: deliver me from the hand of mine enemies, and from them that persecute me!

(PS. 31:15)

Christians are reminded that Jesus is the "Sovereign Lord, holy, and true." The LORD God is omnipotent and is exalted over all the nations. Human beings do not have any power whatsoever to harm the believers in Christ (the Church), unless God allows it. Likewise mayhem can happen only when it is part of His plan and purpose. God

CONCLUSION

is holy and true, so His plan would be good for His people. Those who face persecutions can have peace, knowing that God would allow that to happen if it is good for them.

> *Blessed are they which are persecuted for righteousness' sake: for theirs is the kingdom of heaven.*
>
> (MT 5:10)

> *To him that overcometh will I grant to sit with me in my throne, even as I also overcame, and am set down with my Father in his throne.*
>
> (REV 3:21)

PROFILE OF THE WRITERS

Rev. Dr. Jopie Rattu, DTh, PhD
Education:
1985—Graduated from the Bible School
1988—Master of Arts (MA)
1990—Master of Divinity (MDiv)
1997—Doctor of Ministry (DMin)
2007—Doctor of Theology (DTh)
2010—Doctor of Philosophy (PhD)
Position:
Director of Lembaga Rekaman Injil Indonesia (LRII) since 1979
Lecturer at Tiranus Bible College since 1990
Chairman of Church Representatives and Christian Association (PGPK) in 2006–2015

Sridadi Atiyanto, PhD
Education:
1979—Graduated from the Bible College
1986—Master of Divinity (MDiv)
2011–Doctor of Philosophy (PhD)
Position:
Chairman of Tiranus Bible College Bandung, Indonesia, in 2011–2015

Drs. Yunus Ciptawilangga, MBA
Education:
1984—Bachelor of English Language
1993—Master of Business Administration
Profession:
Entrepreneur in restaurants and technology of information

CPSIA information can be obtained
at www.ICGtesting.com
Printed in the USA
LVHW080512070320
649283LV00003B/5